THE GOLDEN BOO
VIENNA

220 Colour illustrations

BONECHI VERLAG STYRIA

Vertrieb
für Österreich
VERLAG STYRIA
Schönaugasse 64
A-8010 GRAZ

für Deutschland
AZN
Hooge Weg 71
D-47623 Kevelaer

für die Schweiz
Herder AG Basel
Muttenzerstraße 109
CH-4133 Pratteln 1

© Copyright
Casa Editrice Bonechi
Via Cairoli 18/b
50131 Florence, Italy

Printed in Italy by
Centro Stampa Editoriale Bonechi

ISBN 3-222-11752-7

* * *

Vienna during the Turkish siege of 1683
(Georg Philipp Rugendas, Monastery of Heiligenkreuz).

HISTORY

As the Romans marched northwards hoping to extend the frontiers of the Empire all the way to the Elbe river, they reached the site of the present-day city of Vienna. At the time it was inhabited by a Celtic peoples who had dominated the area four or five centuries earlier, replacing an older Veneto-Illyrian population. Recent excavations in the area have brought to light objects from the Neolithic period, proof of the fact that people were already living here 3000 years before the birth of Christ. As soon as the Romans realized the strategic importance of the Celtic settlement, they built a fortified military camp. The powerful Xth legion was stationed here for three centuries, beginning with the middle of the 1st century A.D. The name of the camp, Vindobona, may derive from the Celtic word Vindomina, or Vindo, which means white and which probably alludes to the city's ancient splendor. The specific task of this encampment was to defend the province of Pannonia from incursions by the warlike nomad Quadi tribe. It was situated at the northwest corner of what now includes the
Graben, the Tiefen Graben, Naglergasse, Rotgasse and Kraemergasse. Emperor Marcus Aurelius died here in 180 A.D. Not only had he led the war against the Marcomanni, but he had also found time and inspiration to write a good part of his Meditations. *Upon his death the barbarians whom the emperor had sought to keep at bay were free to overflow the entire region. Between the 5th and 7th centuries, the Danubian plain in all its length and breadth was the theater of barbarian incursions. Ostrogoths, Vandals, Huns, Slavs, Avars poured into Pannonia in successive waves. The destiny of the region and of the city changed in 791 when Charlemagne founded the Western Empire and created the Ostmark, the Eastern March, which was to constitute the principle nucleus of Ostarrîchi, the future Österreich, or realm of the East. Wenia, the new name of the city, also appears for the first time in a document from Salzburg in 881. The Ostmark was ceded in 976 by Emperor Otto II to Count Leopold I of the Babenberg dynasty, thus making him the first hereditary*

margrave in Austria. The region was now independent and the city flourished under this dynasty thanks in great part to its fortunate location on the Danube. It immediately became an important river port and a large trading center, situated as it was on the amber route. Long long ago, before the birth of Christ, merchants had already been carrying amber to the southern parts of Europe. Under Henry II called Jasomirgott (who transformed the Austrian March into a hereditary duchy) the city rose to the rank of residence when the duke moved his court there from Klosterneuburg. The Babenberg dynasty ended with Frederick II and in 1282, after a period of anarchy and struggles, the city passed under the dominion of Rudolf I, founder of the Hapsburg family which was to rule over Austria for almost six centuries. These then were the beginnings of Vienna and as the city grew in size it grew in beauty. The Cathedral of St. Stephen already dominated the city from on high. The first university had already been founded. In 1438, under Albert V, Vienna became the capital of the Holy Roman Empire and the Hapsburg dynasty attained the imperial rank which it was to hold until 1806 when Napoleon abolished the Holy Roman Empire a thousand years after its inception. The only brief interruption occured in 1485 when Matthias Corvinus entered the city at the head of the Hungarian army and occupied it until 1490. The old fortified settlement was a thing of the past and Vienna was now a city of imperial status, subject to no one but the emperor, with a wealth of churches and a flourishing vital culture. When Maximilian I mounted the throne its splendor rose to great new heights. He began the open-minded policy of marriages aimed at acquiring new lands and privileges. His own marriage to Mary of Burgundy in 1477 added Burgundy and the Netherlands to the Empire. In 1496 his son Philip I called the Handsome married Juana called la Loca whose dowry included Castille and Aragon. At the death of the old Maximilian, his grandson Charles inherited everything and became king of Spain under the name of Charles I and emperor of the Holy Roman Empire as Charles V. What better way of realizing the famous motto «Bella gerant alii, tu, felix Austria, nube!» (Others bring wars, you, happy Austria, bring weddings). Thus Vienna found itself the capital of the empire «on which the sun never set» and as such began to play an extremely important role in European history.

It became no less than the last bulwark of western civilization when the Turkish empire, ever more threatening, began to press against the gates of Europe. The Turks, to whom Constantinople had fallen in 1453, invaded Hungary in 1526 and Austria was all that remained between them and the western world. The wars against the Turks exhausted the city which was besieged twice, once in 1529 and again in 1683. Finally in 1697, thanks to Eugene Prince of Savoy, who defeated the Turks at Zenta, the danger was definitively averted. Despite Charles V's repeated attempts to realize a universal monarchy, his hegemonic dream was doomed to failure, unable to withstand the hard blows inflicted by the spread of the Reformation and by the growing affirmation of the principle of the autonomy of the individual nations. Even so Vienna was as resplendent as ever under the enlightened reign of Maria Theresa and then of her son Joseph. The city throve and rivalled even Paris for first place among European cities in the fields of art, culture, politics, and economy. This was the beginning of that «Mitteleuropean» culture which

was to dominate all of Europe until the end of the Hapsburg dominion. When the wars against France were finally over Vienna also became the political center of Europe, and in 1815 played host to the famous congress which attempted to bring peace to the countries that had been lashed by the Napoleonic cyclone. Austria acted as arbiter for European political policy of which Metternich was the chief exponent and took the role of guarantor for all the sovereign states of the conservative reactionary trend which aimed at repressing the movements for liberation and autonomy of the individual populations. A final golden age for Vienna was the reign of Francis Joseph, when the city was modernized and embellished. It now really looked like an imperial city and, most extraordinary of all, the population rose from 360,000 to more than two million inhabitants, making it the largest urban center in central Europe. But the fall of the Austro-Hungarian monarchy was not far off. Despite the enlightened reign of so many monarchs, despite their patronage, above all of music which was queen of the arts for two centuries (the 18th and 19th centuries), despite the creativity of so many geniuses, the milieu in which Vienna and the empire existed was splendidly but extremely delicately balanced. The period of Francis Joseph's long reign was only apparently stable. Actually the empire was slowly crumbling away under the weight of too many different nationalities divided by contrasting interests. The tragic revolver shots fired at Sarajevo were the spark that set off the ultimate cruel tragedy of the Hapsburg Empire. The city's age of splendor came to an end. When in 1918 the Republic of Austria was proclaimed, Vienna was relegated to being nothing but the simple capital of a small country. In addition to the enormous problems that the impoverishment and misery left by the war had created, Austria now found itself suddenly deprived of the many ethnic groups (Czechs, Poles, Croatians, Slovenes, Magyars) which had up to then been subject to the Hapsburgs. But the identity crisis through which the country was passing had not yet reached its nadir. In 1938 Austria and Vienna met their inevitable fate.

Incorporated into the German Third Reich, Vienna hoped for a moment to relive its imperial role once more but it was soon clear that the supremacy of Berlin did not allow for decentralization of this sort and so the city also lost its role as capital of a federal state. Occupied by the Russians in April, 1945, it was subject to a quadripartite Allied administration. Although it was less severe than that of Germany, the allied occupation of Austria lasted ten long years. During this period, with Renner and Korner as presidents, thanks to the contribution of politically middle-of-the-road and moderate currents, the country succeeded in laying a solid foundation for its reconstruction. When the occupation came to an end in 1955, Vienna was once more the theater for the signing of a treaty. On May 15, in the Palace of the Upper Belvedere, the agreement was ratified which restored full sovereignty to Austria, averting any claims the Hapsburgs might still have and guaranteeing perpetual neutrality. The city, which had already repaired a good part of the war damages, was now able to look at its future, at its problems, with renewed hope. No longer an imperial capital, but an equidistant pole of attraction, with solid economic foundations and an efficient administration, Vienna has once more regained the serenity and gracious living for which it is famous throughout the world.

HOFBURG

Time has never stopped in the Hofburg. It is as important historically today as it was in the distant 13th century when the central group of buildings, now known as the Schweizertrakt, was built. The Hofburg is not one single monument but a complex of buildings, squares, courtyards and gardens.

As official residence of the Hapsburgs for seven centuries, it was continuously subject to modifications, carried out in the styles of the different periods. These changes (primarily extensions of the wings and extant premises) cover a period of time that goes from the 16th to the 19th century. Despite this, the Hofburg has managed to maintain a surprising unity, at least from the historical point of view.

Possibly the best way to enter the Hofburg is by way of the Michaelerplatz, on which the main facade of the building, the **Michaelertrakt**, faces. When the exterior of the palace remained to all purposes unfinished

after the construction of the wing of the record office, Emperor Francis Joseph ordered Ferdinand Kirschner to construct a new facade. Kirschner re-elaborated an old project by J.E. Fischer von Erlach and finished the building between 1889 and 1893.

In the shape of a hemicycle, with a high rusticated base and coupled pilaster strips, each end of the Michaelertrakt has a grandiose and animated fountain. The one on the left represents *Austria's Dominion over the Sea*, by Rudolf Weyr (1895), and the one on the right, *Austria's Dominion over the Earth*, executed in 1897 by Edmund Hellmer.

The central part of the facade which projects slightly is completely engaged by a large vestibule covered with a copper dome. Sculptural groups in marble by Lorenzo Mattielli, representing the *Labors of Hercules*, scan the three entrances, while the central portal is decorated with an imposing wrought-iron transenna. This entrance leads into an internal courtyard, known as **In der Burg**, rectangular in shape and enclosed on all sides by Renaissance and Baroque buildings

The elevation of the Hofburg overlooking Michaelerplatz.

which belong to the Alte Burg, or Old Palace. In the center rises the *monument to Emperor Francis I*, erected by the Milanese sculptor Pompeo Marchesi between 1842 and 1846. On the base of the monument, statues of Peace, Might, Faith, and Justice.

Facing the entrance towards the south is the **Leopoldinischertrakt**, which takes its name from Emperor Leopold I, who had it built between 1660 and 1670. The rooms, now official residence of the Federal Chancellor — and therefore not open to the public — owe a large part of their charm to Maria Theresa. One of them was the bedroom of this great empress, and still today one can see the hook attached to the ceiling, corresponding to the bed, with a pulley to which the cord was fastened which was used by the empress in getting herself into a sitting position.

5

The presence of Maria Theresa can still be felt elsewhere as well. Her strong personality unaccountably conquered the Viennese and subjugated statesmen and valid military leaders, who stood at her side. Her spirit continues to live among the common people for whom she remains «die Kaiserin», the Empress. The title, to which she actually had no right, was attributed to her when her husband, Francis of Lorraine, was elected emperor in an attempt to make his true role as prince consort more bearable. It is no accident that at the time it was reported that «the husband of the queen has become emperor». In effect, Maria Theresa was the archduchess of Austria and queen of Hungary and Bohemia, yet her ability was such that her husband's subaltern role never bothered him, or at least it never seemed to. In his memoirs Casanova says he turned his back «on the city and its bigot empress». Actually, at least in her youth, Maria Theresa was anything but a bigot. The difficult moment in history in which she rose to the throne and the enemies who were doing all they could to take it from her quickly tempered her. Yet she never lost her great sense of humanity. An example is her behavior during the terrible plague of 1763 in which, after having lost two sons, she lovingly cared for her daughter-in-law until she too died, catching the disease herself and risking her own life.

Next to the Leopoldinischertrakt, towards the northwest,

Hofburg: monumental entrance on the Michaelertrakt.

Hofburg: left, fountain with «Austria's Dominion over the Sea»; right, «Austria's Dominion over the Earth».

is a short wing called the **Amalientrakt**, characterized by a pleasant octagonal tower covered in copper. Its name derives from the empress Amalia, wife of Joseph I, who lived there during her long widowhood (1711-1742).

The wing on the north, facing the Leopoldinischertrakt, is the so-called **Reichskanzleitrakt**, by J.E. Fischer von Erlach, who built it between 1726 and 1730, commissioned by Emperor Charles VI. The main body of the building, which overlooks the Schauflergasse, is by Lukas von Hildebrandt. Used as a residence for authorities or illustrious guests of the Empire, from 1806 on, it was the abode of the Imperial Chancellery (record office) from which it takes its name.

The rooms which are open to the public are in this wing of the palace. All of them are of interest, but particularly so are *Francis Joseph's bedroom*, with its simple bed, a sign of the Spartan attitude which marked the emperor's private life; his study with the desk over which all the problems of the empire literally passed; and, in the apartments of the empress Elizabeth, the room with the gymnastic equipment used daily by this beautiful woman so obsessed by the care of her body. Other rooms of particular note: the so-called «*Red Room*», completely furnished in Rococo style (the *Gobelin tapestries*, a gift of Marie Antoniette, were made after designs by François Boucher), which was used as a reception hall by Czar

Hofburg: Monument to Francis I.

Hofburg: the internal court known as «In der Burg».

Hofburg: polychrome plaque with the insignia of the emperor Ferdinand I.

Hofburg: the Schweizertor.

Alexander I in the period of the Congress of Vienna, and the *dining room*, still set for a «family meal» according to the canons of Spanish etiquette, which Francis Joseph insisted on rigidly respecting.

The imposing presence of the last great Austrian empress can still be clearly discerned in many places and expressions of Viennese life.

The Austrian poet Alexander Lernet Holenia once told the story of how, when the first sovereign of the Hapsburg dynasty entered the Austrian capital at the end of the 13th century, the Viennese exclaimed «It won't last!». But, concluded the poet, it lasted till 1918. For more than six centuries the Hapsburgs were in the spotlight of European history — 693 years of governing. The reign of

Francis Joseph is one of the longest in history — to be precise, the second after that of Louis XIV. In fact, the Austrian emperor reigned for all of 68 years, from 1848 to 1916. Despite this, Francis Joseph's long reign coincided with the slow but inexorable decline of the dynasty, of which he himself saw the end approaching. In addition, his government suffered serious defeats, as in 1859 with the loss of Piedmont which was aided by the French, or in the Austro-Prussian War of 1866 (not to speak of World War I, of which, it is true, the aging emperor never saw the end, even though he foresaw the outcome). Yet when Francis Joseph married the young and beautiful «Sissi», as Elizabeth was popularly called, in the Augustinerkirche, no one would have thought that the lives of these two sovereigns were to be so full of drama and sorrow.

The wedding itself was marred by two ill omens. Francis Joseph's sabre almost fell when the shoulder belt suddenly gave way, and Elizabeth's diadem got caught for just an instant in the decorations of the coach from

which the newly married bride was descending. These two episodes were interpreted by observers as signs that the emperor would lose his sword and power and that the empress would wear a crown of thorns, with a life of mourning and grief. All of which came to pass.

The emperor's brother, Ferdinand Maximilian, died at the hands of a firing squad in Mexico; their son Rudolf, heir to the throne, committed suicide in Mayerling with Maria Vetsera in dramatic circumstances; the other heir, Archduke Francis Ferdinand, was assassinated at Sarajevo, with his wife Sofia Chotek, and his death set off World War I. Francis Joseph outlived his wife, who was stabbed in Genova by an anarchist.

Hofburg: Francis Joseph's bedroom ▶ (above) and Elisabeth's dressing room (below).

On the following pages: the portraits of Francis Joseph and of Elizabeth by Franz Winterhalter (1865).

Hofburg: the Red Room.

Hofburg: the dining room. ▶

But she had actually already long left her husband and her kingdom, frenetically travelling all over Europe as if she were trying to escape an unpredictably tragic destiny.

On the east the courtyard is closed off by the facade of the wing known as **Schweizerhof**, or Swiss Court, because it was guarded by Maria Theresa's Swiss troops. This section of buildings is the oldest part of the Hofburg and references appear in documents of 1279.

In fact, it corresponded to the medieval castle, defended by four powerful towers at the corners — which it kept until the 18th century — and it was constructed at the wish-es of the first Babenberg sovereigns. Around 1479 Frederick III began to transform and improve it, and Ferdinand I (circa 1530) transferred his residence there. From then on, up to the 19th century, it was the object of continuous changes.

A marvelous Renaissance portal (*Schweizertor*) leads into the Swiss Court. It was probably by the architect Pietro Ferrabosco and contains polychrome coats of arms, inscriptions and frescoes on the underside of the arch and in the passageway. The inscription of 1552, over the portal, commemorates Emperor Ferdinand who began the renovation of the castle.

This part of the Hofburg, too, was the residence of members of the imperial family until the 19th century. The last inhabitant was Rudolf, who lived in the wing entered via the columned staircase.

On the facade, to the left of the Schweizertor, is a fine polychrome plaque (1536) with two griffins holding the insignia of Leopold I.

SCHATZKAMMER

Entrance to the Schatzkammer (Hapsburg Imperial Treasury) is from the Schweizerhof through an entrance situated under the stairs that lead to the Burgkapelle. The collection contains objects of inestimable artistic and historical value, including all the insignia of the Holy Roman Empire and of the Austro-Hungarian Empire.

The jewels of the Order of the Golden Fleece, or of the Dukes of Burgundy, which came to the Hapsburgs by way of the marriage between Maximilian of Austria and Mary of Burgundy, are to be seen here. The *cradle of the King of Rome*, Napoleon's son, is on exhibit and the pitcher and basin used for imperial christenings, fine Italian works of 1571 in solid gold, are jealously conserved.

Among the many precious objects is the *gold embroidered mantle* which Emperor Francis I wore in 1830 for the coronation ceremony of his son Ferdinand, King of Hungary.

This mantle was part of the paraphernalia of precious symbols which belonged to the Austrian Empire, proclaimed in 1804 by Francis II — who for the occasion changed his name to Francis I — in his attempt to save the ideal of the institution, while the German Holy Roman Empire was disappearing under the blows of the Napoleonic forces. But the greatest glory of the Imperial Treasury is the *crown of the Holy Roman Empire*. For a thousand years the peoples of Europe venerated it as the symbol of the power and absolute sovereignty of the German princes. Of gold, with enamel and precious stones, it was made in 962 in Reichenau for the coronation of Otto I.

It was then placed on the heads of all the emperors of the Holy Roman Empire until 1602, when Rudolf II had his craftsmen in Prague make him another *imperial crown*. Thereafter the older one was used only for the coronation ceremony.

Schatzkammer:
crown of the Holy Roman Empire.

Schatzkammer:
imperial crown of Rudolf II.

Schatzkammer: ▶
Mantle of the emperor Francis I.

Studded with diamonds, rubies, pearls and with a sapphire at the summit, in its form this crown recalls medieval models, of the type often depicted in paintings and frescoes. The four reliefs in gold repoussé show Rudolf as a general and his incoronations in Frankfurt, Bratislav and Prague. It must not be forgotten that the Austrian sovereigns were, at that time, emperors of the Holy Roman Empire, kings of Bohemia and kings of Hungary. The scene visible in the photo of the crown shows Rudolf receiving the crown of the Germanic Emperor in Frankfurt.

MICHAELER-KIRCHE

The imposing Hofburg acts as a backdrop for the small intimate Michaelerplatz. Vienna is full of contrasts like this, in which the most majestic expressions of the imperial style are often found side by side with the timid expressions of a style that is both bourgeois and civic. It is on this modest square that the Michaeler-kirche (St. Michael's Church) was built, with the original edifice apparently dating to the 13th century.

Even if it has been altered time and again, the original choir and the slender octagonal Gothic tower, terminating in a spire, are still intact.

The 18th-century facade is preceded by a small portico, with the statue of the *Archangel Michael* executed in 1725 by Lorenzo Mattielli.

The **interior**, although it maintains its original Gothic structure of a nave and two aisles with polystyle piers and tall thick-ribbed vaults, was boldly modified at various later times,

◀ *Michaelerkirche: exterior.*

◀ *Michaelerkirche: interior.*

Michaelerkirche: high altar.

especially in the choir where the sculptural decoration transfigures the architectural structure of the church.

The interior of the choir was transformed in the second half of the 18th century when M. Unterberger executed the group with the *Fall of the Rebel Angels*, a glittering tangle of clouds and bodies, in stucco and alabaster.

The *high altar*, which can be con-sidered the last work of the Viennese Baroque, was created in 1781 by J.B. d'Avrange who used evangelists and candle-holding angels sculptured by J.M. Fischer as decoration.

CALVARY

On the right side of the church, access to which is through a covered passageway in the old house known as Michaelerdurchhaus, stands a large polychrome Calvary, in relief, from the late Gothic period, given to the church in 1494 by the notary and chancellor Hans Hueber. In the foreground Christ is seen praying on the Mount of Olives while in the background the other scenes of the Passion culminate in the Crucifixion. A haunting dramatic composition which recalls the Great Calvaries of Dürer and in general of German painting of the 15th century.

Stallburggasse.

Calvary on the side of the Michaelerkirche.

STALLBURGGASSE

The bell tower of the Michaelerkirche dominates a picturesque group of buildings. The many transformations a city as old as Vienna has been subject to in the course of centuries have played an important part in the formation of views like this. However the presence of antique stores and of the typical handicraft shops and the relative peace and calm of life in this, as in other neighboring old streets, gives an authentic touch of life to what would otherwise be only a time-worn oleography.

The courtyard of the Stallburg.

STALLBURG

Right across from the famous Spanische Hofreitschule in Reitschulgasse, are the Stables (Stallburg), one of the outstanding examples of Renaissance architecture in Vienna.

The building was commissioned by Leopold VI for the successor to the throne and future emperor Maximilian II and was erected between 1558 and 1565 on the site of what was once Babenbergerplatz. Originally separated from the rest of the palace, it is practically square in plan, with the external facades of a classic Renaissance style, sober and without ornamentation. The internal court, however, reserves a pleasant surprise: three tiers of magnificent loggias with open arcading, very close to the best architecture of the Italian Quattrocento. After his coronation, Maximilian II moved to the Hofburg; his residence was turned into the Court Stables and was used as such until 1725 when the stables were transferred to the new building on Messeplatz, now headquarters for the Viennese fairs. Only the best horses used in the Spanish Riding School remained in the Stallburg.

JOSEFSPLATZ

In the course of centuries the area of this square has been used for various purposes. It was first an Augustinian cemetery, then the grounds for a riding school, and later it became a park in accordance with the wishes of Ferdinand I. Emperor Charles VI, as part of a program to complete the Hofburg, had the court Library built there and the area came to be known as Bibliotheksplatz. Joseph II had a wall which ran along the street demolished and thus opened the area to the public. In 1807, with the erection of his *equestrian statue* — by the hand of Franz Anton Zauner — the square acquired its present name.

A charming unified area, it is surrounded by 18th-century buildings. At

the back is the most important, the **old Court Library**, today Austrian National Library, designed by the omnipresent Johann Bernhard Fischer von Erlach and finished by his son Joseph Emanuel between 1723 and 1735. The statues at the top are by L. Mattielli.

Inside, the grandiose *Prunksaal* (now Library Hall) is particularly striking. Two stories high, it occupies the whole length of the palace. The room has a central rotonda and branches off into two long arms. It is richly decorated with allegories which celebrate the glories of the House of Hapsburg. At the center of the rotonda, under a dome frescoed by Daniel Gran with the *apotheosis of Charles VI*, is a statue of Charles in Roman attire. Sixteen other statues

Josefsplatz.

National Library: the Prunksaal. ▶

of emperors, by Paul and Peter Strudel, can be seen set between the columns which articulate the space.

The collection of the Court Library, begun by Maximilian I, includes an impressive number of incunabuli, manuscripts, music scores, papyruses and geographical maps.

Opposite the library, at number 5, is the fine **Palais Pallavicini**, built by Johann Ferdinand von Hohenberg in 1783 on an area originally occupied by other rooms of the Augustine monastery. The portal with caryatids is the work of Franz A. Zauner.

SPANISCHE HOFREITSCHULE

Everyone knows how much the Hapsburgs loved horses. When the English king Edward VII visited Francis Joseph in 1909, proud of his new automobile, the Austrian emperor was not in the least convinced by this new means of locomotion and continued to prefer his horse, Florian.

As early as 1580 Archduke Charles of Styria had had the idea of founding a court stable, its seat in Lipizza, a village in the region of the Carso, which bred horses that were a cross between Arab and Berber stallions and Andalusian mares. With the First World War and the fall of the Austro-Hungarian monarchy, Lipizza was ceded to Italy and the stables were transferred to Piber, near Graz.

Lipizzaner horses are still being bred in Piber today. These highly spirited horses are prevalently white and heavy boned with sinews of steel.

The idea of a riding school in Vienna goes back to 1592, when a wooden building called Spanische Reitschule or Spanish Riding School was constructed for the purpose. At the time only horses of Spanish stock were used, just as nowadays only those of Lipizzaner stock are employed.

An imperial ordinance of 1681 decreed the construction of a permanent riding school. The *Winterreitschule* (Winter Riding School) was begun in the Hofburg in Vienna in 1729 and completed on the 14th of September, 1735.

Joseph Emanuel Fischer von Erlach designed the building with a large luminous white hall with two galleries divided by 46 Corinthian columns and a vault decorated in stucco.

The hall was meant to serve many purposes and in fact torneos, celebrations, festivals and banquets were held there. Among the most important were the banquet on the occasion of the marriage by proxy between Napoleon and Maria Luisa and the balls given during the Congress of Vienna. On the wall opposite the entrance a large portrait of Charles VI riding a Lipizzaner horse catches the eye. Here in these evocative surroundings the real protagonists are the horses: here, to the sound of music, the Lipizzaner horses execute difficult and surprising exercises, such as «courbette» and the «kapriole», under the guidance of and ridden by their equally surprising riders.

Two figures of the riding school: Piaffe (on the left) and Levade (on the right).

AUGUSTINER-KIRCHE

Unfortunately considerable restoration has altered the nature of this church which was originally Gothic. For a long time it was the court parish church and numerous ceremonies took place here. Built between 1330 and 1339 after a plan by Dietrich Ladtner von Pirn as the church of the Augustine monastery it was the object of a series of decorative transformations, as was often the case, and at the end of the 18th century little remained of the austere spirit of a mendicant order. At this point Johann Ferdinand von Hohenberg (1784-85) intervened and the church was stripped of its baroque decoration and at least in part restored to its original simplicity.

Among the ceremonies which took place there, apart from the numerous funerals, including that of Emperor Francis Joseph, mention can be made of the magnificent weddings of Maria Theresa and Francis Stephen of Lorraine (1736); of Marie Antoniette and Louis XVI, celebrated by proxy in 1770; of Maria Luisa and Napoleon, represented by proxy by his former enemy Archduke Charles (1810); of Francis Joseph and Elizabeth of Wittelsbach (1854); and finally the wedding of Rudolf with Stephanie of Belgium (1881).

The most important monument in the church is the tomb of the *Archduchess Maria Christina*, wife of Duke Albrecht von Sachsen-Teschen and daughter of Maria Theresa, which Antonio Canova erected between 1797 and 1805. In its simplicity, its restrained melancholy and serene grief, it best expresses the great Italian sculptor's Neoclassic style. Virtue, Felicity and Charity make a somber pilgrimage into a white pyramid of Carrara marble.

The **Herzgruft** (Heart Crypt) was built next to the church in 1634. It holds 54 urns containing the hearts of members of the royal household.

Augustinerkirche: interior.

Augustinerkirche: the tomb of the archduchess Maria Christina of Sachsen-Teschen (Antonio Canova).

ALBERTINA

On the abutment of one of the antique bastions of the city stands the palace which contains a collection of graphic art, ranging from the Middle Ages to our times, that is truly unique in the world. The watercolors, prints and drawings are all part of the famous Graphische Sammlung, known above all for its collection of prints and drawings by Dürer. The building dates to 1781, but it was enlarged from 1801 to 1804 by Louis Montoyer for Archduke Albrecht von Sachsen-Teschen, son-in-law of Maria Theresa.

On the terrace stands the equestrian statue of another Albrecht von Teschen who defeated the Italian troops at Custoza during the third war of independence and who was to all intents the last of the great military leaders of the Hapsburgs.

The Neo-Baroque *Fountain of the Danube* (Danubius-brunnen) is set against the sustaining buttress of the terrace. It was built in 1869 by Moritz von Löhr, with allegorical statues by Johann Meixner, including the figure of the river Danube with the protected Vindobona.

Albertina: water-color drawing by Albrecht Dürer.

NEUER MARKT

The square of the New Market, originally called Mehlmarkt or flour market, is one of the oldest in Vienna and dates to 1200.

Of the elegant houses in typically bourgeois style which surround it, the most striking is the characteristic facade of a dwelling built in the first half of the 18th century. Seriously damaged during the war the square is now no longer what it used to be.

At the center of the square is what is universally held to be the most beautiful fountain in the city, the *Donnerbrunnen* or Providentia Fountain.

It was realized in 1739 by Georg Raphael Donner. During restoration work in 1873 the lead sculpture was replaced with copies in bronze. The originals are now in the Museum of Baroque Art in the Lower Belvedere.

At the center, four putti play around a pedestal on which is the statue of Providentia. Along the edge of the basin are allegorical representations of the four tributaries of the Danube: the Enns, the March, the Traun and the Ybbs.

Despite the fact that chronologically the figures still belong to the Baroque, they are superbly restrained, modelled with a masterful elegance, with the eye and mind of an artist who had doubtless assimilated the lesson of Classic art.

◀ *The equestrian monument to the Archduke Albrecht over the Danubius-Brunnen.*

◀ *Monument to the victims of Nazism.*

Neuer Markt.

Donnerbrunnen.

KAISERGRUFT

To enter the Kaisergruft (Imperial Crypt) under the Capuchin church is to move through more than 300 years of history. It is here that one finds the 144 tombs of the members of the house of Hapsburg, including 12 emperors and 15 empresses.

The vast complex of the crypt is composed of various chambers which were gradually enlarged and created from 1633 up to 1909. In the old crypt we find the tombs of Leopold I and Joseph I and the haunting tomb of Charles VI, designed by Balthasar Ferdinand Moll, with the lovely sculpture of *Grieving Austria* by Johann Nikolaus Moll.

B.F. Moll also designed the imposing double sarcophagus which contains the bodies of Maria Theresa and her husband, Francis I of Lorraine. The couple is shown reclining on their tomb. At the corners are the crowns of the Holy Roman Empire, Bohemia, Hungary and Jerusalem.

The sarcophagus was made in 1753 when the imperial couple was still alive. When she became a widow, Maria Theresa spent many nights alone next to this sarcophagus which contained her beloved Franz. It must have been a frightening place, full of coffins and illuminated only by the light of the flickering torches. Yet the grief of the empress for the loss of her consort, whom she had sincerely loved, was so great that she was probably unaware of her surroundings.

In the new crypt are to be found the tombs of Francis II and of Maria Luisa, Napoleon's second wife, empress of France and duchess of Parma.

Other tombs set next to each other as if they embodied some sort of tragic symbolism, are those of Francis Joseph, who died in 1916, of his wife Elizabeth, assassinated in Geneva in 1898 by the anarchist Luccheni, and of one of their sons, Rudolf, the heir to the throne who committed suicide in Mayerling in 1889.

All the tombs except one belong to members of the imperial family. The exception is the tomb of Countess Fuchs, Maria Theresa's governess. The empress wanted her faithful friend to repose not far from her more illustrious mistress.

The Capuchin church.

Kaisergruft: the sarcophagus of Francis Joseph flanked by that of Elizabeth (on the left) and of Rudolf (on the right).

Kaisergruft: double sarcophagus with the ▶ mortal remains of Maria Theresa and Francis Stephen of Lorraine.

KÄRNTNER-STRASSE

Literally Carynthia road, it was the principal route southwards as early as the Middle Ages. Through Semmering pass it led to Carynthia and the Adriatic coast. This conferred a decidedly commercial aspect to that part of the Innere Stadt (inner city) through which it went and which became an important point of arrival for goods coming in from the south.

Closed to traffic in 1974, it constitutes a vast pedestrian zone together with the Graben and St. Stephen's square. It is extremely lively, above all at night when thousands of colored lights go on. Elegant shops, famous fashionable cafes and hotels, banks and business offices are at home here.

STEPHANSDOM

The Cathedral of St. Stephen, Vienna's finest Gothic gem and the most beautiful Gothic church in all of Austria, stands in the heart of the old Baroque city. According to tradition, it was consecrated as a parish church in the diocese of Passau sometime between 1144 and 1147. As such, it was outside the city walls, for the center of Vienna then consisted of a square called Am Hof, where the Babenbergs had built their castle.

All that remains today of the original Romanesque building from the first half of the 13th century is the facade with its severe lines. In the center is the famous door built in 1240 and known as *Riesentor* (Giant's Doorway). The rich symbolic decoration in the splays includes busts of the Apostles, figures of animals, grotesques and geometric reliefs, and representations taken from the Apocalypse.

The name of the portal is justified by a curious legend. During the excavations for the foundations of the portal the large fossil tibia of a mammoth came to light. It was hung on the architrave where it remained for a long time and was said to have come from the leg of a giant who had drowned in the Flood. In the tympanum, Christ enthroned between two angels.

The polygonal towers with one-light windows, known as Heidentürme (Heathens' Towers), flank the Romanesque facade which harmonizes with the rest of the Gothic church.

The large south tower looms up at the end of the south transept. It was completed in 1433 under the direction of Hans Prachatitz. The principal landmark of Vienna, this imposing slender tower, 137 meters high, is a typical example of Austrian Gothic. It is called «Steffl», or little Stephen, by the Viennese who must have trembled when it threatened to collapse in the fire that raged through the church after the bombing of April 11, 1945. The tower miraculously resisted but the fate of the marvelous timber vaulting and the fantastic polychrome tiled roof with its fish-scale pattern and a colossal two-headed eagle with spread wings was marked.

Kärntnerstrasse.

The Haashaus, by Hans Hollein.

*St. Stephen's Cathedral ▶
(Stephansdom).*

Stephansdom: Blessing Christ, detail of the Riesentor.

Stephansdom: the Kapistrankanzel.

Stephansdom: Rudolf IV and the standard-bearer, detail of the Singertor.

Stephansdom: interior. ▶

The Baroque organ with 90 registers and the carved stalls of the Gothic choir were also doomed. So was the glorious «Pummerin» (Boomer) the bell which weighed 20 tons, and which had been cast in 1711 by Achamer with metal from the cannons taken from the Turks in 1683. It crashed from its high tower and was smashed to bits.

It was the largest bell in the country, the symbol of Austrian resistance against the invader. The Viennese obstinately made up their minds to reconstruct it when the restoration of the entire cathedral, which was to last until 1952, was begun.

The new bell was cast in Linz, utilizing the fragments of the old bell and bronze that each of the Austrian *Länder* or provinces offered, and was placed in the north bell tower.

Stephansdom: the Dienstboten-Madonna.

Self-portrait of Anton Pilgram in the base of the pulpit.

The base of the organ, with Anton Pilgram's selfportrait.

Stephansdom: the rich decoration ▸ of the pulpit. In the panels are busts of Doctors of the Church: Jerome (left) and Ambrose (right).

This second tower, which was never finished, was begun around 1450 by the architect Puchsbaum who intended to give the cathedral twin bell towers. The work dragged on until 1511 when the Viennese turned their energies elsewhere what with the approach of the Lutheran reformation and the threat of the Turks.

A walk around the church, starting at the right, leads us first to the tomb of the *Minnesinger*, Neidhart Fuchs, under a baldachin, and then to the *Singertor*, which was once a door reserved for men as opposed to the door on the other side of the cathedral which was used by the women. That part of the church came to be called Frauenchor. Protected by a Gothic portal, the Singertor is richly decorated with statues. To be noted is the figure of Rudolf IV, founder of the church, who holds a model of it in his right hand.

On the other side of the apse is the

Stephansdom: Oexl baldachin with the
Madonna of Pötsch.

Stephansdom: the baldachin
by Hans Puchsbaum.

...stiny decided, for perhaps we would
not have been able to do justice to
all his virtues). 73 — a great age for
...at the age of 73 — the average life span

...nel with a
...Eugene
...g Turks, by

...Carignan
...by, in Paris
...663, in Cardinal
...ge of Cardinal
...Louis XIV's,
...ie Savoie-Ca-
...ie adolesc
...his premature d
...fall from
...683, durir
...to serve th
...after an iro
...Vienna, ar
...ces of Leo
...an import
...d his role o
...began to ove
...fortune. A tr
...years late
...IV wrote: «T
...example fo
...... and) I
...the great
...ed. This was

Ste...
Wie...

various generations has added a confused array of works of art in an attempt to make the church as beautiful as possible.

Let us take a look at some of the most important ones. The Kreuzkapelle or Tirna Chapel is particularly interesting from a historical point of view. It was named for a noble family of the time of Emperor Rudolf IV, thought of more or less as a founder of the Church for in 1359 he initiated the transformation of the Cathedral into its present form. Situated at the beginning of the left aisle, the chapel is closed off by a wrought-iron gate with, above, the insignia of the princes of Savoy and Liechtenstein, enclosed in the Collar of the Order of the Golden Fleece. Inside are the mortal remains of the greatest soldier of fortune and man of state ever in the service of the Hapsburg monarchy: Eugene of Savoy.

The prince rests in a sarcophagus decorated with allegorical figures and coats of arms of the family in gilded

bronze. At the side is a p... bronze relief representi... engaged in battle with t... Josef Wurschbauer (175...

Eugene Prince of Sav... was born on October 8,... to Olimpia Mancini, nie... Mazarin and a friend o... and Eugene Maurice... rignan. The years of... were darkened by the... of his father and the... of his mother. In... audience, he offere... King in his army,... fusal, he fled to... himself in the ser... He soon achieve... sition at court, a... man gradually b... that of soldier of... man of his tim... pentant Louis X... is an inimitable... and statesmen... regret enough... France suffer...

Stephansdom, the Women's Choir: the Wiener Neustadt altar with open front.

◄ Stephansdom: the Tirna Chapel. The crucifix dates to the 15th century while the fresco around it is by Josef Ender (1853).

Kapistrankanzel (Capistrano Pulpit) of 1430 above which is a Baroque high relief of 1737 that represents the apotheosis of the preacher. Indeed, it was from this pulpit that St. John of Capistrano, a Franciscan, preached the crusade against the spreading Turkish menace in 1451.

Interior — The church with its elegant nave and two aisles articulated into bays by clustered piers is a hundred meters long, with a transept and a triapsidal choir with three aisles. The Gothic simplicity of the interior is adroitly broken up and varied by the numerous works of art which it contains. Most of these are in the Baroque style. As is often the case in cathedrals whose origins go back to older times, the religious fervor of

various generations has added a confused array of works of art in an attempt to make the church as beautiful as possible.

Let us take a look at some of the most important ones. The Kreuzkapelle or Tirna Chapel is particularly interesting from a historical point of view. It was named for a noble family of the time of Emperor Rudolf IV, thought of more or less as a founder of the Church for in 1359 he initiated the transformation of the Cathedral into its present form. Situated at the beginning of the left aisle, the chapel is closed off by a wrought-iron gate with, above, the insignia of the princes of Savoy and Liechtenstein, enclosed in the Collar of the Order of the Golden Fleece. Inside are the mortal remains of the greatest soldier of fortune and man of state ever in the service of the Hapsburg monarchy: Eugene of Savoy.

The prince rests in a sarcophagus decorated with allegorical figures and coats of arms of the family in gilded bronze. At the side is a panel with a bronze relief representing Eugene engaged in battle with the Turks, by Josef Wurschbauer (1754).

Eugene Prince of Savoy Carignan was born on October 8, 1663, in Paris to Olimpia Mancini, niece of Cardinal Mazarin and a friend of Louis XIV's, and Eugene Maurice de Savoie-Carignan. The years of his adolescence were darkened by the premature death of his father and the fall from grace of his mother. In 1683, during an audience, he offered to serve the Sun King in his army. After an ironic refusal, he fled to Vienna, and put himself in the services of Leopold I. He soon achieved an important position at court, and his role of statesman gradually began to overshadow that of soldier of fortune. A truly great man of his time, years later the repentant Louis XIV wrote: «This prince is an inimitable example for all rulers and statesmen (... and) I can never regret enough the great loss which France suffered. This was what De-

Stephansdom: Oexl baldachin with the Madonna of Pötsch.

Stephansdom: the baldachin by Hans Puchsbaum.

stiny decided, for perhaps we would not have been able to do justice to all his virtues».

At the age of 73 — a great age for a period in which the average life span was 34 years — Eugene, still active in public life, died in his sleep on April 21, 1736, after an intensive day's work, as was his custom, in which he had presided over still another Secret Meeting, taken part in what we would now call a business lunch and attended the much sought-after salon of the Countess Batthyany.

The true masterpiece of St. Stephen's is the *pulpit* which Anton Pilgram sculptured in pure Gothic forms in 1514-1515. In the balustrade the high-relief busts of the Four Fathers of the Church peer out of their niches, each one a superb

*Stephansdom: the tomb of
Emperor Frederick III.*

psychological characterization, sunk
in thought, or in ecstasy, or imbued
with a profound spirituality.

The canons of the Gothic style have
been perfectly respected. The dyna-
mism which pervades the composition
turns every architectural element into
a self-sufficient piece of sculpture, with
a quivering vibrating vitality all its
own.

The creator of this masterpiece
represented himself twice inside the
Cathedral, in a bracket at the base
of the organ loft in the left aisle and,
as if he wanted to sign his loveliest
work, at the base of the pulpit, under
the openwork staircase, holding his
compass, as if he were looking out
of a window. Indeed this expressive
sculpture has been called «the on-
looker at the window».

The left part of the choir, called
Frauenchor, contains a magnificent
Gothic altar frontal in carved and
painted wood. Commissioned in 1447
by Frederick III for the church of the
Monastery of Viktring, it was later
transferred to Wiener Neustadt —
which is why it is called the Wiener
Neustadt Altar — and later (1883) to
St. Stephen's, where it was not publicly displayed until 1952. In the central panel the Virgin and Child with
SS. Catherine and Barbara; above,
the Coronation of the Virgin; in the
doors, stories from the Life of the
Virgin.

The apse of the south choir contains
another famous work of art: the *tomb
in red marble of Emperor Frederick
III.* Niclaes Gerhaert von Leyden
began the tomb in 1467 but never
succeeded in finishing it. The only
thing he did complete was the figure
of the emperor lying on his sarcophagus and the series of statues in the
socle. The Viennese masters Max
Valmet and Michel Ticher terminated

the work in 1513 with the arcaded
balustrade. The rich decoration in the
socle depicts scenes from the Life of
Christ, while on the upper part a series
of 32 coats of arms represents the
possessions and cities subject to the
Emperor. The total of 240 figures
makes this work one of the two largest
bas-relief funeral monuments extant
today in Austria (the other is the tomb
of Maximilian in the Hofkirche in
Innsbruck).

At the beginning of the right aisle
a delicate Gothic baldachin by Gregor
Hauser (1513), covers a modern altar
where the Pötschen Madonna is exhibited. After it had miraculously
wept, this highly venerated image was
transferred to Vienna from Hungary
in 1697 on the orders of the emperor.

Another Gothic altar with a baldachin, probably by Hans Puchsbaum
and dated around 1448, is situated
at the crossing. The delicate decoration lightens the altar which is otherwise weighted down by the tribune
above, meant for the organ.

DIOCESAN MUSEUM

Like many religious orders in Lower Austria, the Cistercian monks of Zwettl also owned a complex of buildings in Vienna, in this case situated on the Stephansplatz, right next to the cathedral, part of whose treasure is kept there.

Of particular importance is the sculpture collection, the most conspicuous pieces of which include a Deposition, a group in polychrome wood from the middle of the 14th century, the Madonna of Erlach (ca. 1330), the Madonna of Thernberg (ca. 1320), the Carrying of the Cross by Jan Henessen (17th century), a splendid St. Anne and the Virgin by Veit Stoss (1505), which comes from the church of the same name. Note should also be taken of various works by Giovanni Giuliani and the wooden model Johann Lukas von Hildebrandt made for the church of the Piarists.

The most important of the paintings in the Museum is the panel with a portrait of Duke Rudolf IV of Hapsburg, founder of the Cathedral, painted around 1365, which is the oldest painting of German school still extant and which is attributed to H. Vaschang. Other noteworthy works include the triptych from the altar in the church of Ober-Sankt-Veit (1507), a work by Leonard Schäufelein, follower of Dürer; an «Ecce Homo» (1537) by Lucas Cranach the Elder; a Madonna and Child, Jesus before Pilate and the Flagellation by Martino Altomonte; as well as paintings of the Baroque period by Michael Rottmayr, Michael Unterberger and Paul Troger.

The treasury contains outstanding sacred objects and furnishings including two glass ampoules from Syria (ca. 1280 and 1310), Rudolf IV's shroud, reliquaries, monstrances and illuminated missals.

Diocesan Museum: Lamentation over the Dead Christ.

Diocesan Museum: the triptych from Ober-St. Veit.

Diocesan Museum: Syrian vases used as reliquaries.

Diocesan Museum: Deposition (1340). ▶

59 KREUZABNAHME
um 1340

39

GRABEN

Surrounded by prestigious palaces and elegant shops, this plaza in the shape of an elongated rectangle is one of the most important points in the city. The name comes from a ditch which used to be here. Halfway between the Vienna of secular traditions, represented by the Hofburg, and the Vienna of religious tradition, represented by St. Stephen's, the plaza contains what may be the must surprising example of Viennese Baroque: the *Pestsäule* (the Plague Column).

Also known as the Dreifaltigkeits-säule (Trinity Column) it is an ex-voto dedicated to the Trinity by Emperor Leopold I to commemorate the terrible epidemic of the plague of 1679. It was at this spot that the bodies of those who had died of the plague were hastily buried. The first column in wood, by Joseph Frühwirt, was later replaced by the present column in marble, splendid and imposing. Franz Menegatti directed the work, while the design was by Matthias Rauch-miller, with contributions by other artists, including Fischer von Erlach. Above the tall base decorated with reliefs — including one of Leopold I kneeling — is a throng of statues, clouds, putti, angels and symbolic figures. Particularly beautiful and striking is the image of Faith triumphing over the Plague.

This type of «cloud» obelisk was so successful that it was copied over and over and can be found everywhere in Austria.

There is a fountain at either end of the square: the *Josefsbrunnen* at one and the *Leopoldsbrunnen* at the other. Erected at the beginning of the 19th century, they testify to the special place these two saints have always held in the hearts of the Viennese.

Graben.

PETERSKIRCHE

Judging from the Baroque facade of the Peterskirche one would never guess that it was traditionally believed to have been founded by no less a person than Charlemagne himself. The church, which faces on the Petersplatz, on one side of the Graben, was begun in the early 18th century, first by Gabriele Montani and then completed, on a new design, probably by Lukas von Hildebrandt. The latter was responsible for the concave facade, framed on either side by a bell tower, and the lovely oval dome, in a warm copper color with its patina of centuries. But the Peterskirche is striking above all for its rich **interior**, lavishly decorated with distinctively Baroque frescoes and sculpture.

The great oval central space is enlarged by shallow niches with altars, and contains works by various famous exponents of the Baroque style: Martino Altomonte, who decorated two altars, one with a *Holy Family*, a *St. Anthony of Padua*, and the large picture on the high altar with *Peter and John healing the lame man*; Johann Michael Rottmayr, who painted the frescoes in the dome; Antonio Galli Bibiena, who designed the main altar which was then realized by Santino Bussi.

Peterskirche.

Peterskirche: the pulpit by M. Steindl.

On the pillars which frame the choir are two sculptures by M. Steindl (1729): a frenetically gesticulating group representing the martyrdom of the patron saint of Bohemia, *St. John Nepomuk* by L. Mattielli, and a sumptuous pulpit covered by a baldachin with angels and a Holy Trinity by M. Steindl.

41

View of Heldenplatz.

Equestrian monument to Archduke Charles.

HELDENPLATZ

The grandiose Square of the Heroes, once the picturesque setting for imposing parades, was created on the orders of Francis Joseph, who had the bastion of the old fortifications in front of the Leopoldine wing demolished to make room for a Kaiserforum — imperial forum — as an enlargement of the Hofburg.

The project was entrusted to Gottfried Semper and provided for two wings in the form of a hemicycle which began at the Hofburg block and arrived at the Ring which was then being developed. Two large statues were to complete the ensemble which also intended to utilize a gateway built in the time of Francis I. But because of the complexity of the whole, the high cost, and the fall of the Hapsburg empire, it remained unfinished. The west wing was never built. Construction work on the Neue Hofburg began in 1881 under the direction of Semper and Karl von Hasenauer and was finished by Friedrich Ohmann, Emil Forster and Ludwig Baumann in 1913. The facade overlooking Heldenplatz has a high rusticated basement and arched windows which alternate with statues inspired by Austrian history. Above is a high loggia of coupled

Equestrian monument to Eugene of Savoy.

columns. The monumentality and imposing aspect of the entire structure is augmented by the vastness of the square, now strewn with flower beds.

The open space is dominated by two bronze *equestrian statues*, one of Eugene of Savoy, victorious over the Turks, made in 1865 by Anton Dominik Fernkorn, and the other, to the west, of Archduke Charles, Napoleon's adversary at Aspern and at Wagram, made by the same sculptor in 1859. The Viennese say that the sculptor, Anton Fernkorn, committed suicide because after having succeeded in constructing the archduke's horse rearing up and supported only on its hind legs, he failed to get the same result with Prince Eugene's horse and was forced to support it on its heavy flowing tail. It is however nothing but a legend which the Viennese love to tell the gullible tourist. Probably the artist himself wanted the two horses in these monuments which face each other to be different as proof of his skill.

Various important museums are housed in the Neue Hofburg: the Waffensammlung, collection of arms; the Musikinstrumentensammlung, collection of musical instruments (16th-19th centuries); the Ephesus Museum, with the reliefs from the Mausoleum of Lucius Verus; and the Ethnographic Museum.

WAFFEN-SAMMLUNG

The most conspicuous part of the collection (Arms and Armor Collection) comes from what Archduke Ferdinand of Tirol had assembled in his castle in Ambras in the 16th century.

A passionate collector of precious objects of all kinds, but interested above all in weapons, the archduke employed two secretaries to organize the research of the numerous agents who were in charge of finding the objects. As a result we have a voluminous collection of letters which document the requests, pressures, flattery used by Ferdinand in his attempts to obtain weapons or armor that belonged to royal personages or famous soldiers of fortune. It has thus been possible to attribute almost every piece in the collection to its original owner. Contrary to the archduke's will, after his death most of the collection was transferred to Vienna and dispersed in various collections.

The *suits of armor* which belonged to sovereigns such as Maximilian I (c. 1550), Charles V and Rudolf (c. 1575) are of particular interest.

Today the collection, which has been enlarged and enriched, is part of the collections of the Kunsthistorisches Museum, even though it is exhibited in the rooms of the Neue Hofburg.

Waffensammlung: armor from the beginning of the 16th century.

Waffensammlung: tournament armor belonging to the Palatine Elector Frederick I (Milan, ca. 1450).

HELDENTOR

Known also as Burgtor, it closes the scenographic Heldenplatz towards the Ring. Conceived of as a monumental entrance to the imperial palaces by Luigi Cagnola and Pietro Nobile, who erected it between 1821 and 1824, it stands on the site of the smallest ramparts of the old city wall. In 1933 it was transformed into a memorial to Austrian national heroes of the war of 1914-1918, in line with a project by Rudolf Wondracek, and received its current name.

BALLHAUSPLATZ

Some of the country's most important administrative buildings face on this square whose name derives from the imperial hall where a type of ball game was played. Besides the *Amalienburg*, they are the old «Geheime Hofkanzlei», which houses the *Bundeskanzleramt* (Federal Chancellery), and the *residence of the President of the Federal Republic*, in the short side of the Leopoldinischertrakt (Leopoldine wing).

The Chancellery was built in 1717-1719 after a plan by Johann Lukas von Hildebrandt and was later (1766) transformed by Nikolaus Pacassi. With the passing of time, the areas liberated by the demolition of the Minorite monastery buildings were used for additions. Today, together with the state archives (Austrian National Archives), the complex of buildings occupies a whole city block.

Great statesmen such as Kaunitz and Metternich worked in the Chancellery and historical meetings were held here during the Congress of Vienna (1814-1815). It was also here that the chancellor, Dollfuss, was assassinated in 1934.

Heldentor.

The facade of the Leopoldine Wing of the Hofburg overlooking Ballhausplatz.

VOLKSGARTEN

Laid out by Ludwig Remy between 1819 and 1823 in concomitance with the development of the area formerly occupied by the bastion of the Hofburg, the Volksgarten today is contiguous with Heldenplatz.

A typical garden in the Italian manner, it contains the so-called *Theseustempel*. This reproduction of a classic Greek temple was built between 1820 and 1825 by the architect Pietro Nobile to house a sculptural group by Canova which represents Theseus killing the Minotaur and which has since been transferred to the staircase of the Kunsthistorisches Museum. The architect's inspiration for the building was the Theseion Hephaestaion on the agora of Athens and he created a hexastyle peripteral structure in Doric style, with six columns on the front and trabeation.

Volksgarten: the Theseus-Tempel.

Volksgarten: the monument to the empress Elizabeth.

The small Theseus temple and the *monument to the Empress Elizabeth* in the western corner of the garden have something in common. Elizabeth had a passion for Greek antiquities which explains her predilection for the island of Corfu, one of the stopping places in her restless flight from the oppressive court.

The monument, designed by the architect Friedrich Ohmanns and executed by the sculptor Hans Bitterlich, was unveiled on June 4, 1907.

BURGTHEATER

Built between 1874 and 1888 on designs by Gottfried Semper and Karl von Hasenauer, it was inaugurated with Schiller's drama «Wallensteins Lager». The bombardments of the last war did not spare the theater. A raging fire, in 1945, largely destroyed it but fortunately stopped short of the two wings, so that it is still possible to see the marvelous *frescoes* by Gustav Klimt and Franz Matsch on the vaults over the staircases.

Restoration was undertaken after the war under the direction of Michael Engelhart and the Burgtheater opened once more in 1955 and from then on it has occupied a fundamental place in the theater circuit of Vienna and of Europe.

Burgtheater.

Burgtheater: the interior staircase.

DREIMÄDERLHAUS

The so-called House of the Three Sisters stands at Screyvogelgasse no. 10, halfway up the slope of the Molker Bastei, the remains of one of the fortifications of the city. Built in 1803, it is an excellent example of Biedermeier style, a disparaging term which passed into normal usage at the beginning of the 20th century with reference to the style of life characteristic of the period of the Restoration in Germany.

Biedermeier, a word resulting from the juxtaposition of the adjective *bieder* (honest) and the common German surname Meier, was originally the name of an imaginary master with which the poet Ludwig Eichrodt signed a long series of ironic verses, written between 1850 and 1857 for the satirical newspaper «Fliegende Blatte» (Flying Sheets). The Biedermeier man, rather simple-minded and limited, stops trying to solve important problems and withdraws into himself, attempting to reconcile the ideal with the real in the cult of nature and small everyday things.

Even though completely without a historical basis, the house is popularly attributed to the memory of Franz Schubert and the three sisters Hennerl, Hederl, and Heiderl, daughters of the glazer Tscholl, who figure in the operetta «Dreimäderlhaus».

This romantic story tells how the penniless musician spent much of his time in the salon of the three Fröhlich sisters — who owned the house at the time — to play on the piano, which he didn't have, as well as to enjoy the comforts offered.

VOTIVKIRCHE

Built between 1855 and 1879 along the lines of French Gothic cathedrals of the 13th century, the Votivkirche was commissioned by Maximilian, brother of Emperor Francis Joseph, after the latter escaped an attempt on his life by the anarchist Libeny in 1853. The costs of the construction were covered by a subscription opened in 1856 in which over 300,000 citizens took part.

Its daring neo-Gothic structure is the work of the architect Heinrich von Ferstel, who had just turned 27 and who had designed the University. Two towers, 99 m. high, terminating in spires, flank the facade with its fine rose window.

RATHAUS

Modelled on the town hall of Brussels, the Vienna Rathaus looms as one of the most monumental constructions on the Ring.

The palace was erected between 1872 and 1883 after designs by Friedrich von Schmidt, who was called from Cologne as architect for St. Stephen's cathedral. The neo-Gothic building has a central steeple 100 meters high on top of which is the Eiserne Rathausmann, that is «the

Dreimäderlhaus.

Votivkirche.

Rathaus. ▶

iron man of the city hall», three meters high, by Alexander Nehr (1882).

Up to the middle of the 19th century the site was a vast field for military drills and parades. Cajetan Felder, the mayor at the time, obtained permission from the emperor to transform it into the building zone that we see today.

These were the years of a great new spurt in growth — the Ring, the famous artery encircling the old city, had just been built on the site of the old walls —, and the transferral of the municipal offices into more spacious quarters could no longer be postponed.

The whole area thus became an «administrative center», with a new University as well as City Hall and Parliament.

PARLIAMENT

The first Austrian parliament to be elected was the so-called «Kremsierer Reichstag», created after the revolt of 1848. Nonetheless, it was not until 1870 that the assembly became democratic in the modern sense of the term. The building which faces on Dr. Karl Renner Ring is where the two houses of the Austrian Federal Assembly (the Bundesrat and the Nationalrat) meet.

The Danish architect Theophil von Hansen drew inspiration for his Vienna Parliament Building from a long sojourn in Athens. Erected between 1874 and 1883, its projecting central pavilion has eight Corinthian columns surmounted by a pediment, and two wings, also with columns, which terminate in two smaller temples.

Everything here is the triumph of Classicism: the fine monumental fountain in front of the building, representing Pallas Athena, set up by Karl Kundmann in 1902; the four bronze statues of horse tamers, sculptured by Lax; the seated statues of Greek and Roman historians.

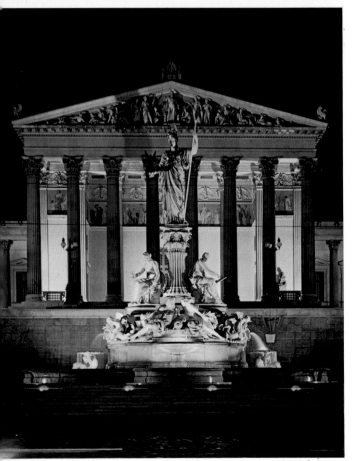

Parliament palace.

The fountain with Pallas Athena in front of the entrance to the Parliament palace.

50

KUNSTHISTORISCHES MUSEUM

The enormous Maria Theresienplatz which was created around 1870 as part of the development project of the Ring is the Viennese center for museums. In the middle of the square is the *monument to Empress Maria Theresa* erected in 1888 with bronze statues by Kaspar Zumbusch — Maria Theresa is seated on her throne and is surrounded by her counselors (standing) and her generals (on horseback), Laudon, Daun, Khevenhüller and Traun.

The two symmetrical buildings of the Naturhistorisches Museum (Museum of Natural History) and the Kunsthistorisches Museum (Museum of Art) face each other across the square. They were built between 1872 and 1881 by Gottfried Semper and Karl Hasenauer in a typically Italian Renaissance style. They are identical, each with a tall dome, a balustrade decorated with statues of famous men and a long facade with columns and engaged pilasters. The Natural History Museum is one of the richest and most complete museums of its kind in the world. Among its numerous finds from the Iron Age is the famous *Venus of Willendorf*. The Kunsthistorisches Museum, on the other hand, is universally acknowledged to house one of the most important collections of art in the world, above all as far as the picture gallery is concerned.

The imposing facade of the Kunsthistorisches Museum.

The monument to Maria Theresa.

51

who preferred Venetian painting, an inventory of 1659 listed as many as 1400 works of art temporarily housed in the stables of the imperial castle. With the Archduke's will of October 9, 1661, all this wealth was assigned to his nephew Emperor Leopold I, into whose hands an immense inheritance of art treasures finally found its way. In fact, in addition to the gallery of Prague, his paternal inheritance, he also received the collections in Vienna and in Innsbruck.

Once everything had been transferred to Vienna, the problem of where to install works arose, for the collections continued to grow in the times of Maria Theresa as well as in those of Joseph II. Not until Francis Ferdinand was a definitive collocation of the various collections under a single roof planned and it was then that the present Kunsthistorisches Museum on the Ring was built.

The Picture Gallery occupies the first floor, while collections of other arts are on the mezzanine. All kinds of

Staghunt of Elector Frederick the Wise, ▶
by Lucas Cranach the Elder (1529).

Hunters in the Snow, ▶
by Pieter Bruegel the Elder (1565).

Emperor Rudolf II, by Hans von Aachen (ca. 1595).

Theseus and the Minotaur, by Antonio Canova.

The history of the Vienna picture gallery is quite complex and is essentially the story of the Hapsburgs who collected these paintings. In the time of Maximilian I (1459-1519), a collection of portraits already existed, even if it could not yet be considered a real true picture gallery. The portraits were of interest more from a genealogical point of view than for any particular artistic quality they might have. His successor, Archduke Ferdinand II (1529-1595), also concentrated exclusively on «portraiture», but during the seventeen years of his lieutenancy in Bohemia (from 1547 to 1563), he laid the foundations of a larger collection which in later centuries was transferred to Ambras, near Innsbruck.

At the same time, in the other capital of the Hapsburg empire, Prague, Rudolf II (1552-1612) was collecting paintings just as passionately, availing himself of the art collections of other members of his family as well. He acquired the collection of the castle of Ambras when Ferdinand II died in 1595 and he also appropriated the most outstanding works in the collection of his brother, Archduke Ernest. During his lieutenancy in the Netherlands (1593-1595), the archduke had come into the possession of many works by Flemish painters. Had it not been for the good taste and passion of this prince of the house of Hapsburg, the Vienna museum would today be without its most prized nucleus, the many paintings by Pieter Bruegel the Elder. The archduke was the first to understand them and to love them — the first to buy them.

The collections passed into the hands of various successors, one after the other, growing in size and importance. At the time of Archduke Leopold William (1614-1662),

precious objects are on exhibit here: from bronzes to goldwork, from tapestries to ivories, as well as Egyptian, Greek, and Roman antiquities, all of them there thanks to the munificence of the Hapsburgs.

Let us mention, for example, the imposing Egyptian sarcophagus in black granite of the Ptolemaic period; the funerary chamber, complete with its furnishings, of Prince Kaninisut, from Giza; the Roman bronze copy of a Greek original known as the Ephebus of Magdalensberg, from the place in Carynthia where it was found; the sardonyx cameo, known as Gemma Augustea, representing the triumph of the emperor Tiberius. Outstanding the section dedicated to sculpture, with numerous splendid examples of Italian Renaissance sculpture in addition to the Krumauer Madonna. And then of course there is the famous salt cellar in gold which Benvenuto Cellini made around 1540 for Francis I of France.

Among the painters represented in the Picture Gallery particular mention should be made of Van Eyck, Bruegel the Elder, Van Dyck, Rubens, Rembrandt. And for the Italian school: Titian, represented by many works which document his whole career, and Giorgione, Veronese, Raphael, Caravaggio.

◀ *Vienna seen from the Belvedere, by Bernardo Bellotto (1759/60).*

◀ *Pietà, by Annibale Carracci.*

Statue of the Pharaoh Thutmosis III (18th dynasty, ca. 1450 B.C.).

Marble head of the goddess Artemis (3rd to 1st cent. B.C.).

The Ptolemy Cameo (3rd cent. B.C.).

Virgin and Child,
by Tilman Riemenschneider (ca. 1510).

Laughing Boy, by Desiderio
da Settignano (ca. 1455).

Salt cellar,
by Benvenuto Cellini (1540/43).

BURGGARTEN

The fortifications which enclosed Vienna were rather out of date when, in 1809, perhaps on psychological rather than strategical grounds, Napoleon had the ramparts in front of the imperial palace blown up. This furnished an occasion for the enlargement of the palace and the embellishment of the area. The result in 1820 was the Burggarten, or gardens of the Hofburg. At the edge of the park, on the Ring, right after the Theater, is the *monument to Goethe*, erected by Hellmer in 1900. Other statues, commemorative monuments to great Viennese, are inside the park, half-hidden in the green: *Mozart*, previously set up in the Albertinerplatz, dated 1896, is by Viktor Tilgner, and the one to *Francis Joseph*.

Burggarten: the monument to Mozart.

Monument to Goethe.

Burggarten: the monument to Francis Joseph, by J. von Klimbusch (1908).

STAATSOPER

The construction of the Staatsoper (Opera House), one of the principal lyric theaters in the world, was begun immediately after the opening of the Ring. The competition for the project was won by the architects Eduard van der Null and August von Siccardsburg, who were inspired by the forms of the early French Renaissance, adding a more typically Viennese and monumental character. Begun in 1861, the Opera House was solemnly inaugurated on May 25, 1869, with Mozart's «Don Giovanni».

But neither of the architects lived to see this ceremony. A mildly negative comment on the part of the Emperor Francis Joseph regarding the proportions of the facade had so hurt Van der Null that he hanged himself and Von Siccardsburg died two months later, overcome by grief.

The Opera was almost completely destroyed by the aerial bombardments of March 1945, and was rebuilt under the direction of Erich Boltenstern. After its restoration the exterior of the theater remained as it had been, with a portico facade, while the interior was considerably modified and furnished with up-to-date technical equipment. The Opera reopened in 1955 with Beethoven's «Fidelio», almost contemporaneously with the Burgtheater.

The **interior** is magnificently ornate: the auditorium has over 2200 seats, the double staircase is decorated with *statues of the Muses* by Josef Gasser and the ceiling lunettes with *frescoes* by Moritz von Schwind, from 1867, in which scenes from Mozart's «Magic Flute» are represented.

The famous «Opernball» is held here in January or February. The pit is then transformed into a single magnificent ballroom. That evening imperial Vienna magically comes back to life in all its pomp and splendor.

MUSIKVEREINS-GEBÄUDE

Designed for the Gesellschaft der Musikfreunde (Society of the Friends of Music) by the architect Theophil Hansen, the evident neoclassical reminiscences include spaces articulated by pilaster strips and a triangular pediment in the gable. One of the principal centers of musical life in Vienna, it was built between 1807 and 1869.

The heart of the building is the large concert hall or «Hall of Gold»

Facade of the Staatsoper.

Musikvereinsgebäude: the Gold Room.

with a capacity of 2042 spectators, richly decorated with stuccoes and caryatids. In 1911 the painter August Eisenmenger frescoed Apollo and the Muses in some of the panels of the coffered ceiling. It is from this room,

where Bruckner's six symphonies had their premiere, that the famous New Year's Concert, played by the Vienna Philharmonic, which has its head-quarters here, is broadcast throughout the world.

The Archives of the Society, founded in 1812, have a wealth of manuscripts including the original of Beethoven's Third Symphony («Eroica») and Mozart's Concert for piano in G flat.

59

PALAIS TRAUTSON

This palace (Museumstrasse 7) is perhaps the most important private building in Vienna designed by the famous architect Johann Bernhard Fischer von Erlach. Begun around 1710 under the direction of Christian Alexander Oedtl, on the commission of Prince Trautson, it was terminated in only two years. The building has a solemn grandiose facade, crowned by a pediment that immediately recalls neoclassic taste, emphasized by the portal with its three arches, the three large windows and the sculpture above the balcony. The stucco decoration in the gable depicts Olympus. Two sculptured sphinxes and four giants which support the consoles of the vault, works which can probably be attributed to Giovanni Giuliani, decorate the monumental staircase. Maria Theresa bought the palace in 1760 and it then became the headquarters of the sovereign's Royal Hungarian Guard, which continued to be stationed here until World War I. Since 1972 Palais Trautson has housed the offices of the Federal Ministry of Justice.

PALAIS LIECHTENSTEIN

The Stadtpalais Liechtenstein with its monumental four stories set around a square internal court was built between 1694 and 1706 to designs by Domenico Martinelli, who had received the commission from Count Kaunitz. Shortly after work was begun, it was acquired by Prince Johann Adam Liechtenstein who set the architect Gabriel de Gabrieli at Martinelli's side.

The main facade of the palace on the Bankgasse in particular betrays the influence of the Roman Baroque of Fontana and Bernini, while the elevation on the Minoritenplatz is very close to the style of J.B. von Erlach, especially in the portal decorated by imposing caryatids and atlantes (*Venus and Vulcan* by Giovanni Giuliani).

Inside, the splendid staircase of honor has a ceiling frescoed by Antonio Bellucci and is decorated with stuccoes by Santino Bussi and sculpture by Giovanni Giuliani.

Between 1836 and 1845 the interior of the palace was radically transformed in Rococo style, but its original Baroque aspect was restored in 1976 when the heavy war damage was repaired.

Minoritenkirche: the apse.

Minoritenkirche: interior.

Minoritenkirche: pediment of the west portal with the Crucifixion by Master Jakobus.

Palazzo Trautson: the interior staircase.

Palais Liechtenstein: secondary entrance with the Atlantes, by Giovanni Giuliani.

MINORITENKIRCHE

At the center of the tranquil Minoritenplatz stands the national Italian church of Vienna, the Minoritenkirche, so-called because it was founded in the 13th century by an order of minor friars.

Largely destroyed by fire, reconstruction of the church was begun some time around 1350 and it was later enlarged, remodelled, restored. It does however still preserve its fine Gothic plan and the twin portals on the facade, decorated with a *Crucifixion* carved around 1350 by the monk Jakobus, as well as the slender octagonal tower which rises at the apse and which is known throughout Vienna because it is docked. In fact the spire was demolished in a bombardment during the siege by the Turks in 1683.

The **interior**, restored to its Gothic forms between 1784 and 1789 by Johann Ferdinand von Hohenberg who removed the Baroque transformations, is solemn and beautifully simple. With a nave and two aisles, all the same height supported by tall piers, it is a typical hall church. At the end of the right aisle is the *commemorative monument of Pietro Metastasio*, court poet under Charles VI and Maria Theresa, who died in Vienna in 1782.

The *high altar* is also noteworthy. It was made in 1781 by Jean B. d'Avrange and has rich stuccoes. A point of curiosity is a large mosaic executed at the beginning of the 19th century by Giacomo Raffaelli, on Napoleon's commission, reproducing Leonardo's *Last Supper*.

The monastery attached to the church was demolished in 1881-1909 to make room for public buildings.

FREYUNG

In the Middle Ages the monastery of the Scots, which stood here, guaranteed the right of sanctuary to all, from whence its present name, Freyung. The vast square is adorned in the center by the *Austriabrunnen* (Austria Fountain), with allegoric statues of the Danube River, the Vistola, the Elbe and the Po, by the hand of Ludwig von Schwanthaler. The *Schottenkirche* (Church of the Scots) dominates the square. It was founded in 1155 by Henry II Jasomirgott (margrave and duke between 1141 and 1177) for the Scottish and Irish Benedictine monks who came from Regensburg. The church was modernized in Baroque form from 1638 to 1648 by Andrea d'Allio and Silvestro Carlone. The attached monastery contains a rich picture gallery of works by 18th-century Austrian painters. Right opposite the Schottenkirche is the *Palais Daun-Kinsky*, a Baroque ma-

Palais Daun-Kinsky: exterior.

Freyung Square.

Kirche «Am Hof».

The Zeughaus, the old arsenal of the city.

sterpiece by Lukas Hildebrandt, who built it between 1713
and 1716 for Count Philipp Daun. It was later bought by
Prince Kinsky. The Baroque, which came to Vienna late,
is a dominant aspect of the city. The heavier characteristics
gradually precipitated, giving way to a relative simplicity
and sincerity that take one's breath away.

AM HOF

In the Middle Ages this was the real nerve center of
the city. The name of the square refers to the fact that
the court, or Hof, was established here at the time of
Henry II Jasomirgott. This sovereign, whose nickname
refers to his habit of exclaiming «May God help me!»,
succeeded around 1156 in transforming the March of
Austria into a hereditary duchy. Thanks to him, the country
became politically autonomous and enjoyed considerable
economic prosperity. In one corner of the square rises
the old city arsenal, the *Zeughaus* built around 1550, but
remodelled in 1731 and 1732 in its present form. The robust
statues which decorate it and the two-headed eagle on
the facade are by Lorenzo Mattielli. Also on the square
is the *Kirche am Hof*, or Church of the Nine Angelic
Choirs, dating to 1386 but transformed into Baroque forms
at the beginning of the 17th century. The facade, which
consists of a porch surmounted by a terrace, is by the
Italian architect Carlo A. Carlone, and is from 1662.

It was from this church that Pius VI, the only pope to
have visited Vienna in the past, imparted the benediction
«to the city and the world» in 1782.

ALTES RATHAUS

The first town hall in Vienna was probably located not far from the Altes Rathaus (Old Town Hall), in the nearby Tuchlaubenstrasse, the name of which refers to an old family of cloth merchants. In the 13th century the honor of housing the municipal authorities passed to a palace, the core of the present Altes Rathaus, that was confiscated from the powerful Haymo von Neuburg family.

In 1309 an uprising against the Hapsburgs, who had dominated Vienna since 1276, broke out, organized by the aristocracy and the merchant middle classes. The revolt was put down and the property of those who had dared rebel was confiscated. The powerful Otto Haymo saw his patrimony go up in smoke and Frederick the Fair, symbol of the entire dynasty, in 1316 gave the confiscated house of Otto to the city of Vienna.

The palace was frequently enlarged in the centuries to follow and it was totally renovated in Baroque style in 1706, until 1885 when the new palace on the Ringstrasse was completed. At this point the old Rathaus ceded its post as town hall and more modestly continued to house various administrative offices.

The facade on Wipplingerstrasse, which dates to between 1699 and 1707, betrays the influence of Johann B. Fischer von Erlach. On the piers of the two portals, pairs of statues allegorically represent the civil virtues: at no. 6 Justice and Generosity (1706) and at no. 8 Devotion and Public Faith, the latter by Johann Martin Fischer.

The famous Andromedabrunnen (Andromeda Fountain) is in the picturesque courtyard. It was made in 1741, for the civic administration, by the sculptor Georg Raphael Donner. For this, which was his last work, he executed an imposing bas-relief in lead, with Andromeda in the foreground, a prisoner of the Dragon who will fall under the blows inflicted by Perseus, shown advancing from the deep perspective of the background. Two pairs of putti support the balcony above, decorated with an ornate balustrade in wrought iron, by Simon Vogel (1725).

Inside the palace, the fine 18th-century stuccoes which decorate the stairs and the later stuccoes (19th cent.) in the Council Hall are worthy of note.

BÖHMISCHE HOFKANZLEI

The Bohemian Chancellery had its headquarters in this palace. It stands in front of the Altes Rathaus and was built between 1708 and 1714 on designs by Fischer von Erlach. The architect Matthias Gerl enlarged it between 1750 and 1754: the additions are to be seen in a large part (about half) of the facade on the Wipplingerstrasse, while the entire facade on the Judenplatz is to be ascribed to Gerl, who, however, faithfully copied the architectural elements set into the palace by Von Erlach. Further modifications, both outside and inside, were carried out during the 19th century. Later it had to be partially reconstructed (1951) as a result of war damage. The majestic portals with Atlantes supporting the heavy trabeation, decorated with statues by Lorenzo Mattielli, make this facade one of the finest examples of the Viennese Baroque. At present the Constitutional and Administrative Court has its seat in the palace.

◄ *Altes Rathaus: the facade.*

Altes Rathaus: the Andromedabrunnen.

Böhmische Hofkanzlei:
facade on Wipplingerstrasse.

HOHER MARKT

The Hoher Markt is the oldest square in Vienna, originally dating back to the Roman conquest. In fact this was where the Roman «praetorium» was situated, and where the emperor Marcus Aurelius probably died in A.D. 180.

The Fountain of the Wedding of the Virgin (Vermählungsbrunnen) rises in the center of the Hoher Markt. It is also known as Josefsbrunnen (St. Joseph's Fountain). It was erected as the result of a vow Leopold I made during the Spanish occupation, so that the successor to the throne, Joseph, might return safe and sound from this difficult undertaking.

The project for its construction was entrusted to Johann Bernard Fischer von Erlach, who initially, in 1706, raised a wooden column on the site of the gallows. The work was modified and finished by his son Joseph Emmanuel, who worked on the present monument from 1728 to 1732: a large bronze and marble baldachin. The figures in marble, which represent the marriage of the Virgin in the presence of the Pope, are by Antonio Corradini. Two basins designed by L. Mattielli complete the monument.

The cold bulk of the Ankerhof, the palace which houses the Anker (anchor) Insurance Company, dominates the eastern corner of the Hoher Markt. An amusing example of the Viennese Art Nouveau, the Ankeruhr, projects from the building out over the Rotgasse. The mechanism of this unique clock, constructed in 1914 to the design of the painter Franz von Matsch, is arranged so that the passage of the hours is marked by the succession of the most important figures in Austrian history inside a charming bull's-eye window in Art Nouveau style.

RUPRECHTS-KIRCHE

Traditionally the church was founded in 720 by the bishop of Salzburg, Vergilius, in honor of St. Ruprecht on the site where the monks

The Vermählungsbrunnen.

Hoher Markt: the Ankeruhr.

Ruprechtskirche: the south side.

Maria am Gestade, interior: Annunciation (1460 ca.).

Maria am Gestade, interior: Coronation of the Virgin (1460 ca.).

Maria am Gestade: the facade. ▶

Chuniald and Gisalrich had erected a house of prayer and meditation.

In any case, it is cited in a document of 1161 as the oldest church in Vienna. The bell tower with two-light windows — the top story was added in the 12th century — and the simple Gothic interior with two asymmetrical aisles on piers and a small polygonal apse are quite stirring.

MARIA AM GESTADE

The name means «Mary on the banks». The banks were those of the Danube which flows along below and the church was built over the spot where the boatmen moored their boats. It was already mentioned in documents of 1158 as a Romanesque sanctuary and was renovated more than once.

The church we now see was built in various stages. The choir and the tower went up between 1330 and 1369, the nave between 1394 and 1414. The fine polygonal tower, terminating in an openwork spire, was built by Michael Knab, the duke's architect, between 1394 and 1427. Damaged during the two Turkish sieges of 1529 and 1683, it was restored in the 19th century when the emperor Francis I gave orders to recuperate the church which was in a wretched state as a result of the French occupation of 1809 during which it was used as a storehouse and military stables.

The statues by the sculptor Joseph Beyer which decorate the gable on the facade and the intrados of the portal were added early in the 20th century.

The interior too is like a small Gothic jewel: a poetic dark narrow nave which terminates in a luminous choir, lighted by fine stained-glass windows dating to between 1350 and 1430. The high altar is an outstanding neo-Gothic work by Thomas Marzik (1846).

A small chapel on the right side of the nave houses part of a triptych painted in 1460 by the Master of Maria Stigen in Dutch ambience which represents the Coronation of the Virgin and the Annunciation.

HEILIGENKREUZERHOF

In the Middle Ages the great monasteries already had their city houses — the so-called Klosterhofe — which were used primarily as warehouses for the products of the monastery which were to be sold in the city market. Gradually these places were transformed into headquarters for the monks themselves.

The Heiligenkreuzerhof — an authentic oasis of peace inside the city — in the oldest part, dates to the time of the Babenbergs and belongs to the famous monastery of Heiligenkreuz, a few kilometers south of Vienna. The simple and solemn aspect of the courtyard is the result of the comprehensive restructuration to which it was subject from 1660 on. The most interesting part is without doubt the Baroque Chapel of St. Bernard (1659-1676) with the large painting by Martino Altomonte which represents the apparition of the Virgin to St. Bernard, and the two groups of sculpture which flank the high altar (Joseph with the Christ Child, and St. Anne teaching Mary), both by Giovanni Giuliani (ca. 1732). The statues of St. Florian and St. Leopold on the high altar are also by this sculptor.

Thanks to their timely transferral to the Heiligenkreuzerhof, many of the abbey's art objects and documents were saved from destruction during the Turkish siege of the city in 1683.

Heiligenkreuzerhof.

The interior of the Bernhardskapelle.

PRIVATE HOUSES

Scattered throughout the old city center are numerous private houses that are of particular interest from an architectural and historic point of view. Many of these buildings are concentrated in the labyrinth of small lanes between the apse of the Cathedral and the Old University.

The Basiliskenhaus, a building that dates all the way back to the 13th century, is at Schönlaterngasse no. 7. The name derives from a curious legend according to which a small dragon, hatched from a hen's egg, was found in a well in front of the house. The inhabitants were unable to free themselves from the dragon, until a young baker petrified him by showing him his image in a mirror. The petrified Basilisk is still to be seen on the facade, but it is a pity that the monster is nothing but a block of sandstone which time and weather have shaped into this bizarre form.

In the adjacent Bäckerstrasse at no. 7, is a late 16th-century house famous for its Renaissance staircase, its forms softened by an age-old climbing vine, while at no. 8 is the former Sailern palace built in 1722 in the style of Hildebrandt.

Not far from here, at no. 8 Domgasse, we can admire the house in which Mozart composed his «Marriage of Figaro». The artist, who lived here between 1784 and 1787, occupied the apartment on the first floor.

Backerstrasse: the Renaissance courtyard of the house at no. 7.

Domgasse: Figarohaus.

Schönlaterngasse: the Basilisk house.

JESUITENKIRCHE

The Jesuit church was erected between 1627 and 1631 at the behest of the emperor Ferdinand II who, in the midst of the Thirty Years War, desired to emphasize the role of the Company of Jesus, a true symbol of the Counter-reformation. Since the management of the University of Vienna was also entrusted to the congregation, the church is also known as the University Church.

Between 1700 and 1705 Andrea Pozzo radically transformed the interior and added the bell towers conferring its present aspect to the building.

The exterior, with its two tall towers flanking the facade, is typically Baroque while the interior of the church is a real triumph of the style of the Counter-reformation.

The richly-decorated nave has trabeated columns at the sides. The altarpiece on the high altar, representing the Assumption of the Virgin, and the decoration of the vault with a large perspective fresco that simulates the presence of a dome, are also by Andrea Pozzo.

For centuries the Ignaz-Seipel Platz, onto which the facade of the Jesuit Church faces, has been the heart of official Austrian culture. The Alte Universität (Old University) had its seat in the building complex that occupies the entire block enclosed by the square, Bäckerstrasse and Postgasse. After the closure of the University of Prague, it was the oldest German-speaking university, deriving from the Studio founded by Rudolf IV in 1365.

The elegant palace which stands across from the Alte Universität is the only example of French classicism in Vienna, commissioned in 1753 by Maria Theresa from the architect Jean Nicolas Jadot, so as to provide the institute with a new spacious hall. The room — now the Festhalle — was decorated with frescoes by the Roman Gregorio Guglielmi, destroyed by fire in 1961 and then replaced by copies by Paul Reckendorfer.

Jesuitenkirche: the facade.

Jesuitenkirche: the pulpit. ▶

POSTSPARKASSE

At the beginning of the century the Austrian government decided to complete the project of the Ringstrasse with the Stuben quarter, along the final stretch of this large thoroughfare. Two large public buildings were planned to make the most of the area; the Ministry of War and the Postal Savings Bank. Otto Wagner, who for some time had been involved in the planning of the whole zone with an imposing mass of detailed projects, participated in the competitions for these two groups of buildings.

He lost the one for the Ministry, for which a much more mannered project was chosen, but he won the one for the bank. With this project he was able to achieve the sophisticated yet essential style, severely elegant, at which he had been aiming for years. Here the architect is not interested in attempting to confer monumentality on the building through the recuperation of stylistic elements of the past, but he achieves his scope through an elimination of lines, the simplification of the design and the use of new materials.

The palace, built between 1904 and 1906 and enlarged in 1912, has absolutely innovative decorative features,

Georg Coch Square with the Postsparkasse. In the foreground the monument to Coch.

such as the marble facing «fixed» with countless nails which are actually unnecessary, for the slabs are properly cemented in place. Although originally Wagner had planned a glass dome, he abandoned this idea and used unusual materials, such as aluminum, in the garlands and statues of the Geni, works by Othmar Schimkowitz.

MUSEUM FÜR ANGEWANDTE KUNST

The first of its kind in Europe, the Museum of Applied Arts first saw the light in 1864 as the Austrian Museum of Industrial Arts, on the initiative of Rudolf von Eitelberger, and its purpose was that of putting into practice the concept then fashionable that Art was to renew the entire sphere of human life, reshaping everything created and utilized by man, until it achieved a total work of art.

Museum für Angewandte Kunst: room dedicated to Art Nouveau furniture.

Museum für Angewandte Kunst: the covered atrium.

For a long time the Museum and the annexed School of Applied Arts played a determining role in the development of esthetic taste in the field of industry in the Austro-Hungarian Empire.

Designed by Heinrich Ferstel in a style that echoes the Florentine Renaissance, and built of unplastered brick which has little or nothing to do with Florentine architecture, it went up between 1868 and 1871 as part of the project for the development of the Ring.

On the wall which connects the Museum to the adjacent College of Applied Arts there is a fountain decorated with mosaics representing Pallas Athena, executed in 1873 by Antonio Salviati, as well as majolica medallions and graffiti by Karl Karger and Ferdinando Laufberger.

The Museum contains a great variety of objects from all over. They range from Romanesque and Gothic textiles to Italian, French, Flemish tapestries and Persian rugs; from European crafts to Chinese objects from the Ming period (porcelain, glass, majolica, lace, goldwork, intarsia). The Museum even contains a Renaissance portal from the Florentine church of Santa Maria Novella.

The collection of furniture is also outstanding: Rococo pieces, examples created by the artists of the Secession and others in Empire and Biedermeier styles.

STADTPARK

The idea for the park originally came from the painter Joseph Selleny and it was laid out — thanks to the mayor, A. Zelinka — during the period of expansion which coincided with the construction of the Ring.

Stadtpark: where the Wienfluss comes out into the open.

Stadtpark: the monument to Johann Strauss Jr.

A picturesque stream, the Wienfluss, runs through the Stadtpark, which also has a small artificial pond and swans and peacocks. Opened in 1862, it is one of the loveliest parks in the city.

The architectural structures along the place where the Wienfluss comes out into the open and on either side of a brief tract along the banks were realized between 1899 and 1907 on a project by Friedrich Ohmann and Joseph Hackhofer. The idea was to turn the surroundings of the small stream into a promenade, particularly once it had been decided to join the adjacent Kinderpark to the Stadtpark.

The park is decorated with numerous commemorative monuments and statues, including one of *Franz Schubert* and the famous figure of

Johann Strauss Jr., the «Waltz King», made by Edmund Hellmer in 1923. The bronze figure of the great Viennese composer, shown playing his violin, is set under a white marble arch decorated with reliefs which represent the dancing waves of his famous «Blue Danube».

A touching homage of the city to its most famous and beloved son: Strauss was a real idol for the masses and his fame surpassed that of the emperor.

The *Kursalon*, a massive pavilion built by Johann Garben between 1865 and 1867, is also to be found in the Stadtpark. It is the site of a café-restaurant and is a kind of temple to the Viennese waltz. Waltz competitions are so frequent that it is legitimate to suspect they are put on for the tourist rather than being real examples of folklore.

The tradition of the café as a place to rest and drink one's cup of coffee while reading the newspaper is one of the characteristics of Vienna which fascinates the visitor.

Stadtpark: the monument to Franz Lehar, by the sculptor Franz Anton Coufal (1980).

Stadtpark: Kursalon.

KARLSKIRCHE

The Karlskirche was built in honor of St. Charles Borromeo in fulfillment of a vow made by Emperor Charles VI during the plague of 1713. It was on this occasion that the emperor had the following inscription set on the tympanum: «Vota mea reddam conspectu timentium Deum». (My vow has been fulfilled in the sight of the God-fearing). Building began in 1716 on plans by J.B. Fischer von Erlach, who won out over Galli Bibiena and Hildebrandt in the competition decreed by Charles VI. At the time the church was on the other side of the Wien river and at the end of a street which began at the Hofburg, so that the facade would have been a sort of perspective backdrop in contrapposition to the imperial palace.

It is said that the idea for the novel facade, with its two enormous freestanding columns in front of the church, came to Von Erlach after he had seen St. Peter's and Trajan's column fused together as one from the Pincio at sunset. Whatever the great architect's inspiration may have been, there is no doubt that there is nothing quite like it. The central part of the facade has a low classical portico at the center with a lofty ovoid dome and a low tower on either side. In front of the facade and almost as high as the dome, as if they were confirming the solemnity and originality of the concept, are two triumphal columns with spiral reliefs depicting scenes from the life of St. Charles Borromeo. The columns are 33 meters high and were executed between 1724 and 1730 by J.B. Mader, J. Schletterer and J.B. Straub. The pediment of the facade is decorated with a low relief by G. Stanetti symbolizing the end of the plague.

In 1722 J.B. Fischer von Erlach interrupted the construction of the church. It was continued by his son Joseph Emanuel who began work on it in 1724 and finished in 1737.

The **interior**, without all the resplendent color contrasts and the extravagance of the Baroque, is sober and harmonious. A single vast oval space is covered by the dome and surrounded by side chapels. In the dome, Johann Michael Rottmayr frescoed *The Triumph of St. Charles*, between 1725 and 1730. Of interest, in two of the side chapels, an *Assumption of the Virgin*, by Sebastiano Ricci, and a *St. Elizabeth* by Daniel Gran. The fine carved benches, which are curved so as to follow the plan of the church, should also be noted.

Karlskirche.

RESSELPARK

The gardens in front of the majestic Karlskirche were begun in 1862 as one aspect of the large city-planning project centered around the Ringstrasse. The vicinity of the Polytechnical Institute suggested naming it after Josef Ressel (1793-1857), inventor of the naval propeller. A monument to him by Anton Dominik Fernkorn was set up in the park. As time went on it was joined by other monuments dedicated to eminent men, above all inventors. One of these is the bust of Josef Madersperger (1768-1850), inventor of the sewing machine, by Karl Philipp.

At the edge of the Park, on Karlsplatz, is the white monument to the composer Johannes Brahms (1833-1897) by the sculptor Rudolf Weyr, which was inaugurated on May 7, 1908. The great German musician, who moved to Vienna in 1863, lived for fifteen years not far from here at Karlsgasse no. 4 and worked in this area as director of the Orchestra of the Musikvereingebäude from 1871 to 1875.

Conscientious and tenacious, but sarcastic and withdrawn, towards the end of the century, with his music, he interpreted deep-seated trends in Viennese society towards the crepuscular style of the «decadents».

Resselpark: Henry Moore's «Reclining Figure».

Resselpark: monument to Brahms by Rudolf Weyr.

The new building of the Polytechnical Institute.

KARLSPLATZ

There is no doubt but that the architect and town planner Otto Wagner (1841-1918) was the initiator of the Austrian renewal in architecture, and his ideas strongly influenced the Secession movement, with which however he himself had little to do. He immediately came to the fore as a thoroughly prepared highly accomplished professional and was the author of important studies for the expansion of the city. Unfortunately the only part of his plans actually realized was the project for the city transportation system which the artist considered the keystone in any town-planning project.

The transportation system was realized between 1894 and 1901 and Wagner, nominated chief engineer of the project, designed more than thirty stations, turning his attention to the placing of viaducts and tunnels and personally designing even the small details such as street lamps, balustrades, and even the lettering. This is why the old Transportation system is, as a whole, considered the architect's masterpiece.

Wagner also took advantage of the occasion to experiment with new avant-garde building techniques and made ample use of iron decoration as well. He even went so far as to use it in the terminus of Schönbrunn (reserved exclusively for the royal family so that they could reach their castle there), where this humble material was ennobled and used in the dome.

Iron is also an important element in the two twin pavilions of Karlsplatz, authentic jewels of the complex. Built in typical Art Nouveau style with marble facing decorated with floral motifs in gold, they were dismantled and completely restored in 1978. While one of them still serves as entrance to the transportation system, the other is used in summer as a Café.

The present layout of the square was overseen by the Danish architect, S.I. Andersson.

THE SEZESSION

In the 1890s young artists who wanted to study painting had to attend the Imperial Academy where imitation of the past was rigidly imposed and innovation was frowned on.

It is therefore no wonder that in the end the students rebelled. Nineteen of them, headed by Gustav Klimt, abandoned the Academy in 1897 and founded the «Vereinigung bildender Künstler Österreich Sezession» (Association of painters and sculptors of the Austrian Secession).

The Secessionists, in line with the artistic revolution begun by the French impressionists, affirmed that the goal of the artist could no longer be the imitation of the past, but the creation of a new style. This idea was synthetized in the movement's slogan: «to each time its own art, to each art its freedom» (Der Zeit ihre Kunst, der Kunst ihre Freiheit).

Sezessionhaus.

«Marcus Antonius», bronze by A. Strasser.

◀ Karlsplatz: pavilion of the
Transportation System.

Klimt, the most important figure in the
movement, always stressed the «freedom» of
the artist, maintaining an anti-doctrinaire
attitude; as a result the works of the so-called
artists of the Secession have no common
identifying characteristics.

This does not mean a lack of program,
for they had both a site for their headquarters
and a publication for the diffusion of their
ideas (the «Ver Sacrum»).

In 1897-98 one of the outstanding members
of the artistic movement, Joseph Maria Ol-
brich, designed this building for the exhibi-
tions of the Secession Group. His particular
love for coloristic effects is evident above all
in the gilt iron *dome* with its openwork pattern of laurel leaves.

Next to the pavilion is Arthur Strasser's
bronze *monument to Marcus Antonius*, of
1899-1900. This work by an artist who had
nothing to do with the movement, placed
next to the Secession temple, testifies to the
old empire's extraordinary capacity for as-
similation with regard to its opponents. The
fact that the emperor himself was present at
the inauguration of the Secession headquarters was not fortuitous.

LINKE WIENZEILE

With the two «Dwelling Houses» designed and built by Wagner on the Linke Wienzeile between 1898 and 1899, the architect once and for all broke with the Ringstrasse models and adopted the ideas of the Secession movement, affirming that the function of a building is what determines its form. This explains why Wagner did not conceal the diverse functions of the rooms on the lower floors — shops and offices — from the living quarters above, but stressed this difference, creating two distinct bands.

The house at no. 40 — the famous Majolika Haus — once more testifies to the artist's preference for new materials: iron for the columns and balustrades and tiles with a lovely floral pattern for the facade.

In the adjacent «rental house» — at no. 38 — he exploited the presence of the corner with Köstlergasse to curve the facade, dividing it into two different elevations, creating a luminous loggia on the top floor.

Wagner, in his personal concept of architecture, tried to unify the value of the apartments as dwellings by installing an elevator — as usual of elegant design — a modern concept destined to replace, to all effects, the old staircase which led only to the first floor.

Majolikahaus: facade and detail.

Linke Wienzeile no. 38: detail and exterior. ▶

PALAIS SCHWARZENBERG

The palace rises behind the monument to the Soviet Army at one end of Schwarzenbergplatz, at the center of which is the statue of Prince Karl von Schwarzenberg who defeated Napoleon in the battle of Leipzig (1813).

Palais Schwarzenberg might almost be called a logical premise to the monumental Belvedere palace next to it which was being built in those same years. With its court of honor, its imposing facades and its position overlooking the center of the city, it is a perfect synthesis of the concepts of two of the most famous architects of the Austrian Baroque: Hildebrandt's elegance and sobriety of line on the one hand and Von Erlach's sculptural sense of form on the other.

In 1697 Prince Heinrich Franz Mansfeld-Fondi had Johann Lucas von Hildebrandt begin construction on his first palace in Vienna. Work was interrupted in the first decade of the 18th century and the unfinished building was bought by Prince Adam Schwarzenberg (1716) who entrusted the continuation to Johann Bernhard Fischer von Erlach (1720-23) and his son Emmanuel, who finished it in 1728.

A monumental staircase with two flights of stairs crowns the central section of the garden facade of the building and leads to the extensive palace gardens laid out by Jean Trehet and considered to be among the loveliest in Vienna. The staircase is preceded by a series of statues by the Italian sculptor Lorenzo Mattielli.

Of particular note inside, where Fischer von Erlach the Elder's sense of imaginative decorativism and attention to detail come to the fore, are the domed hall and the chapel. The building was damaged in the war and remodelled and part of it has now been turned into a hotel. It also contains an interesting picture collection.

BELVEDERE

The entire Belvedere, with its two palaces and the vast garden, an unusual and unique example of a princely abode, was built as a summer residence by Prince Eugene of Savoy, thanks to whom the Turks had been permanently ousted from central Europe in the victorious battle of Zenta. «The emperor in the wings», as he was called for the enormous influence he exerted on the Hapsburg court, had in 1695 already acquired land south of the walls, along the Heerstrasse (now Rennweg), the road that leads to Hungary. Work did not

The facade of Palais Schwarzenberg.

Panorama of Vienna from ▶ the Upper Belvedere.

start until 1700 when the land was terraced for a garden and in 1714 work on the Lower Belvedere began.

The landscape gardener Dominique Girard was called in for the project and the actual work was carried out by Anton Zinner, the Inspector of Parks, who worked on it until 1725.

The gardens, which provide a beautiful view of the city, fascinated numerous artists including the Italian Bernardo Bellotto. They act as a marvelous link between the two buildings of the Belvedere which are the principal works of Johann Lukas von Hildebrandt, one of the greatest names of Austrian Baroque, who succeeded in joining French and Italian experiences to a pure Viennese spirit.

It took so long for the complex to be completed — twenty years passed from the time the land was bought to when construction started — because Eugene lived in relative financial straits. It was in fact not until 1707 (when he was nominated Governor of Lombardy, with an income of 150,000 florins) and then with his nomination as Governor of the Low Countries (June 25, 1716) that the prince had fixed sums of money at his disposal.

Initially only the construction of the **Lower Belvedere** (Unteres Belvedere) was planned. It was built between 1714 and 1716, as can be gathered from indirect references, for the original documents have all been lost together with Prince Eugene's archives.

The palace, as we have said, was to be the prince's summer residence and therefore Hildebrandt designed it as two long simple wings separated by a raised central body.

Particular care was given to the interior decoration and a host of famous and excellent painters and sculptors were called in to decorate it as elegantly as possible.

Currently the rooms of the Lower Belvedere house the Austrian Baroque Museum (Österreichisches Barock-

Lower Belvedere: the garden facade.

Lower Belvedere: the old bedroom ▶ of Prince Eugene. At the center «Apotheosis of Charles VI» by G.R. Donner.

Lower Belvedere: two of the ▶ «character heads» by Franz Xavier Messerschmidt.

museum) with important examples of 17th- and 18th-century works which show off to their best in these contemporary rooms.

Outstanding is the *Marmorsaal* (Marble Room) with its solemn facing in red marble articulated by stuccoes and perspective frescoes by Gaetano Fanti. On the ceiling Martino Altomonte painted one of the three *Apotheoses of Prince Eugene* in the Belvedere.

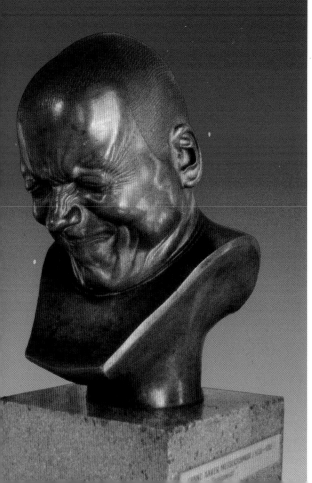

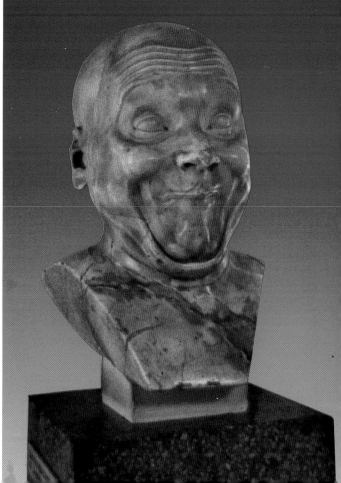

In the fresco, the soldier of fortune, after his victorious battle of Patervaradino (1714), is shown as Apollo guiding the chariot of the Sun. This room houses the lead originals of the statues for the Providentia-Brunnen in the Neuer Markt, made by Georg Raphael Donner in 1737-39.

Another extremely interesting room is the prince's bedchamber (next to the Marmorsaal), still with its original wall covering, where we can also admire two other fine works in marble by Donner: a relief of «Hagar in the Desert» and the large group of the «Apotheosis of the Emperor Charles VI» as well as the bronze reliefs «The Judgement of Paris» and «Venus in Vulcan's Smithy».

In the Room of the Grotesques (which takes its name from the decorative elements in the frescoes by the painter Jonas Drentwett) are kept some of the famous «caricature heads» by Franz Xavier Messerschmidt (1736-1783). Inspired by the physiognomic studies and theories of the Swiss Johann Kaspar Lavater which established a relationship between a man's character and his facial features, the sculptor here has furnished us with masterly examples of this concept.

The adjacent *Marmorgalerie* (Marble Gallery), where the red stone has been used in the form of linear molding which encloses and separates the white zones of the stuccoes and the masses of the statues, contains two other works by Messerschmidt: the lead figures of the empress Maria Theresa and her consort Francis Stephen.

Not to be overlooked is the *Hall of Mirrors*, or the Goldkabinett (so-

Lower Belvedere: the Marmorsaal with the statues of the Providentia Brunnen.

Lower Belvedere: Goldkabinett, the ▶ «Apotheosis of Prince Eugene» by B. Permoser (1721).

called on account of the precious wainscotting, remodeled in Rococo style under Maria Theresa), where another «Apotheosis of Prince Eugene» is on exhibition. This one is in marble, sculptured by Balthasar Permoser between 1718 and 1721, und unanimously considered the apex of Austrian Baroque. It might also be mentioned that the artist portrayed himself in the Turk subjugated by the prince.

Later Eugene decided to take full advantage of the panoramic position and build a castle at the top of the hill. This new structure, the **Upper Belvedere** or Oberes Belvedere, was to be used exclusively for the great receptions and splendid festive occasions which he frequently organized.

The project was once more commissioned from Hildebrandt and was rapidly concluded (1721-1722). The architect, harassed by the urgent entreaties of the prince, complained in a letter to a friend, which has come down to us.

Johann Lukas von Hildebrandt (1669-1745), familiarly known as Gianluca, was born in Genoa and had begun to work with Eugene during the prince's Italian campaign in

◀ *Upper Belvedere: the main facade and the garden facade.*

Upper Belvedere: the «sala terrena» with the Atlantes which support the vault; below: the Marmorsaal.

1695-96, as fortifications engineer. When he returned to Vienna he was immediately given an official position in the Court and rapidly became famous.

The building Hildebrandt designed

consists of two main facades with four octagonal pavilions at the corners and various projecting blocks which render the vast architectural surface more picturesque, and the whole is covered by a characteristic roof in copper. It seems that when «Gianluca» showed Eugene his designs and explained how he wanted, not to build, but to model the castle in the countryside and in the air, the prince exclaimed: «This rhythm is fascinating; you have imprisoned an architectural dream».

This palace, too, was sumptuously decorated on the inside. Gaetano Fanti, Carlo Carlone, Martino Al-

tomonte and Giacomo del Po frescoed the walls, while Santino Bussi provided the elegant stuccoes unfortunately modified in the 19th century. The ground floor vestibule (*Sala Terrena*) is particularly beautiful, adorned with four powerful atlantes who act as pillars and hold up the vault. This architectural solution, which Hildebrandt borrowed from the staircase in Eugene's town palace, where E.B. Fischer von Erlach had used pillars just like this, dates to the end of 1732, when the ceiling of oak panels which had rotted and threatened to collapse had to be replaced.

Upper Belvedere: Admiral Tegetthoff at the Battle of Lissa, by Anton Romako (1880 ca.).

Upper Belvedere: Judith, G. Klimt's first painting of this subject in its original frame (1904).

Upper Belvedere: Portrait of Sonja Knips, by Gustav Klimt (1898).

This is indirect evidence of the haste with which Hildebrandt was forced to work.

Another extremely interesting room is the great marble hall on the first floor, also known as *Marmorsaal*. On the ceiling Carlo Carlone frescoed still another *Apotheosis of the Prince*, a confirmation of the fact that the artist's first task in those days was the glorification of his patron, above and beyond all reasonable limits.

On May 15, 1955, the Österreichische Staatsvertrag (Treaty of State) which brought to an end the ten-year long occupation of Austria by the Russian, French, English, and American allies, was signed in this room.

For the garden in the back, over which the east facade looks out,

Hildebrandt found a unique solution by building an enormous basin, so that the view of the palace, from this side, appeared lower and more elegant.

Upon Prince Eugene's death, the Belvedere was inherited by Victoria of Savoy, who sold the property to the Hapsburg court. In 1777 Emperor Joseph II had the imperial picture collection, which was to become part of the Kunsthistorisches Museum in 1890, installed here. After that, the heir to the throne, Archduke Francis Ferdinand, who was later to be assassinated at Sarajevo, lived here.

Today the beautiful rooms of the Upper Belvedere house the *Austrian Gallery of 19th and 20th Century Art* (Österreichische Galerie des 19. und 20. Jahrhunderts) which includes examples of Austrian art from the early Neoclassical period up to the artistic expressions of our times.

More than any other museum in Vienna, this exhibition documents the painting of the Biedermeier period and of the Austrian Secession. The former is well represented by artists such as Ferdinand Georg Waldmüller (1793-1865), Jakob von Alt (1789-1872), Rudolf von Alt (1812-1905), Friedrich von Amerling (1803-1887), Friedrich Gauermann (1807-1862), Moritz Michael Daffinger (1790-1849).

Next comes a group of works which document the «Idealizing Historical» school of painting, whose greatest exponent, Hans Makart (1840-1884), perfectly interpreted the tendency for pomp and monumentality of the rising middle classes at the time of the «Ringstrasse». A contemporary of Makart, but extraneous to the official style, Anton Romako (1832-1889), particularly skilled in psychological portraits of his sitters, heralded the renewal which was to be introduced by the Secession.

The Gallery has a rich collection of works by the artists of this movement, above all by Klimt (1862-1918).

The section dedicated to contemporary painting vaunts works by Egon Schiele (1890-1918), Oskar Kokoschka (1886-1980), and Herbert Boeckl (1894-1966).

A museum has also been installed in the old *Orangerie* of the Belvedere. The *Museum of Austrian Medieval Art* (Museum Mittelalterlicher Österreichischer Kunst) contains above all 15th-century works of painting and sculpture. Of particular note, among others, are works by Roland Frueauf the Elder, Michael Pacher, the Master of the Altar of Albrecht and of the Altar of the Creation in Vienna.

SCHÖNBRUNN

Schönbrunn like Versailles, the Hapsburgs like the Bourbons. This spirit of rivalry and emulation gave birth to the marvelous complex of Schönbrunn, park and castle, a typical example of the splendor of the Austrian court and the Baroque taste of the period.

As early as the beginning of the 14th century, the monastery of Klosterneuburg owned vast stretches of land in this area, with a fortified mill known as Katterburg.

In 1559 Emperor Maximilian II acquired the estate to use as a reserve and turned the mill into a hunting lodge.

According to tradition, as Matthias — who was crowned emperor in 1612 — was out hunting in the early days of his reign, he happened upon a spring of the purest water which he called «beautiful spring» or «schöner Brunnen».

The hunting lodge was damaged several times before it was finally completely demolished by the Turks during the siege of 1683.

When in 1692 Emperor Leopold I decided to rebuild the palace as a summer residence for his son Joseph, he entrusted the task to his favorite and most important architect, Johann Bernhard Fischer von Erlach, who prepared a grandiose plan with a royal palace which would have surpassed the French royal palace in Versailles in monumentality and scenographic grandeur. The original design, in fact, placed the castle at the top of the hill where the Gloriette now stands, while a system of ramps and terraces gradually moved down to the bottom of the hill.

Precisely this is what would have differentiated it from Versailles. While Louis XIV's royal palace rises above

a large court and via the court is ideally connected to the underlying village, Leopold's royal palace would have been majestically isolated and detached from the secular world. However, despite the period of great prosperity enjoyed by the court, the finances of the Austrian state were not up to vying with French finances, and Von Erlach himself remodelled his plan, completely reversing it. The castle was brought down low, while the park moved uphill as far the loggia which was all that remained of the original idea.

Even so, the concept of Versailles is still there in the vast gardens which, in line with French taste, became architecture, with the radiating avenues which intersect each other, with the

flower beds, the fountains and mythological statues which populate the shady corners.

Work began in 1695 and by 1713 the central body and the two wings were finished. This was followed by a pause due to Charles VI's lack of interest in the palace, until Maria Theresa had the work continued under the direction of Johann Emanuel Fischer von Erlach. In 1774 Nikolaus Pacassi took over the direction of the works, adding a floor to the central body and erecting the columned hall on the ground floor. The new Rococo taste insisted on lightening the emphatic accents and saw to it that all was resolved in an atmosphere of serene humanity, in which the influence of the great empress definitely played a part.

Between 1817 and 1819 the facades were modified, especially the garden facade, in line with a more «classicizing» project proposed by the architect Johann Aman. After the bombings and grave damage inflicted in 1945, a thorough restoration of the castle was immediately initiated which lasted up to 1952.

The facade with its double flight of stairs overlooks the spacious court of honor which is embellished by two basins with fine allegorical groups dating to 1776. On the left are the rivers: the Danube, the Inn and the Enns, by Johann Baptist Hagenauer; on the right, the kingdoms of Galizia, Lodomiria and the principality of Transylvania, by Franz Anton Zauner.

Despite its majestic proportions, an air of restrained and graceful simplicity emanates from Schönbrunn. There is nothing of the exaggerated pomp and unbridled luxury of Versailles.

The 1440 rooms of the palace, now in part used as a museum and in part for offices, are imbued with history. The two marriages of Emperor Joseph II were celebrated here, first with Isabelle of Parma (1760) and then with Maria Josephine of Bavaria (1765). Napoleon Bonaparte, after

Fountain with the allegories of the dominions of the crown, by F.A. Zauner (1776).

Fountain with the allegories of the Rivers, by J.B. Hagenauer (1776).

View into the «Bergl rooms». ▶

Maria Theresa, painting by Martin Van Meytens.

The Hall of the Horses. ▶

The study of the archduke Francis Charles. ▶

The Vieux Laque Room.

The Millions Room. ▶

occupying Vienna in 1805, set up his general headquarters here and then lived in the palace for almost six months in 1809, when the Peace of Schönbrunn was signed. His son, the pathetic and unfortunate Aiglon, king of Rome, whom his Austrian grandfather had rebaptised Duke of Reichstadt, lived and died here. Francis Joseph was born and died in Schönbrunn, and it was also here, on November 11, 1918, that the Hapsburg empire came to an end when Emperor Charles signed his abdication document.

But there is more than just history to the **interior** of Schönbrunn. It has remained practically unchanged since the time of Maria Theresa, with its precious Rococo furnishings, full of gilded stucco, period furniture, tapestries and mirrors.

The simple austerity of the apartment of the last imperial couple seems to have crystallized in time, as has the bare room of Francis Joseph, the «old Emperor», as he was familiarly called by the Austrians.

An initial idea of the beauty of the interiors is provided by the Peacock Rooms — or Bergl Rooms — a series of small rooms on the ground floor of the palace. When some old wall covering was being restored in 1891, imaginative landscapes came to light. They had been frescoed between 1769 and 1777 by the Bohemian artist Johann Bergl, and are typical examples of the Rococo delight in depicting elements taken from the flora and fauna. The rooms were used by Maria Theresa as a cool retreat from the summer heat of the rooms on the upper floor.

The blue staircase leads to the upper floor where the rooms that are open to the public arouse a whole range of emotions. In the *Hall of Horses*, the great care with which the Hamilton brothers, «court painters for the animals», have depicted the best or finest examples in the imperial stables of the time, leaves one speechless. Outstanding is the large canvas with «Joseph I and a Hunting Party», by Martin van Meytens.

One cannot help but be drawn to the relatively simple furnishings in the *study of the archduke Francis Charles*, father of Francis Joseph, with a fine canvas by Van Meytens of Maria Theresa and Francis Stephen sur-

rounded by their children, portrayed on an imaginary terrace overlooking the court of honor of Schönbrunn.

Nor can words describe one's feelings upon entering the *Vieux Laque Room*, with its walnut wainscotting set with black lacquered panels of Chinese landscapes in gold, with gold and stuccoed frames.

The wainscotting, designed expressly by Isidoro Carneval to use the panels which had been bought previously, is mitigated by three portraits of members of the house of Hapsburg.

Two of them were painted by Pompeo Batoni and represent Francis Stephen of Lorraine and his children, Joseph and Peter Leopold, both destined to reign over Austria, and to leave a profound mark in the history of the time. Joseph was shrewd and ambitious and instituted great reforms, at times considered ahead of his time. Peter Leopold, who succeeded him and who abandoned the Grand Duchy of Tuscany after twenty-five years of excellent government, was particularly humane and well-balanced.

But the most precious room is the astounding «*Millionenzimmer*» (Millions Room, so-called because that is what it presumably cost in crowns). Completely paneled in rare Chinese rosewood, the walls are studded with gilded Rococo ornaments which frame 18th-century Indo-Persian miniatures. The marble bust in a corner of the room, representing Marie Antoinette, daughter of Maria Theresa and queen of France when she was sixteen, is by Giuseppe Ceracchi.

Another unusual room is the small round *Chinese Cabinet* — with its oval twin — where Maria Theresa loved to linger and play Faro. Here too the wainscotting has been embellished by the insertion of lacquered panels decorated in gold. Small shelves, with Chinese vases in white and blue porcelain, project from the walls.

The *Grand Gallery*, a vast room of state for the official receptions, is majestic but simple in its beauty — above all if compared with other rooms.

103

Francis Joseph's bedroom.

◀ *The bedroom of
Francis Joseph and Elizabeth.*

◀ *Francis Joseph's study.*

In the ceiling Gregorio Guglielmi allegorically celebrated the glory of the reigning couple in his fresco with the personifications of the subject territories which render homage to the sovereigns at the center, and at the sides the triumphs of war and peace. It is here that Maria Theresa listened to the notes of a concert given by a six-year-old child named Wolfgang Amadeus Mozart.

The rooms occupied by the last «master of the house» Francis Joseph are however in a more homely Biedermeier style. Born here — in a room next to the study of his father, Francis Charles — on August 18, 1830, he lived much of his life in Schönbrunn. The fine painting by Franz von Matsch on the wall of his *study* shows him at 68, at his desk, a meticulous bureaucrat and untiring worker, a real first civil servant.

The adjacent *bedroom* confirms the emperor's Spartan way of life: the simplest kind of iron bed, a chair or two and an ordinary bureau are all the furniture in the room. Francis Joseph died in this very bed on November 21, 1916, after sixty-eight years of reigning spent, because of his pride and the high concept he held of his mission and an exaggerated sense of duty, in a solitude that was far greater than was necessary for a man in his position. The large painting that decorates the room — a work by Von Matsch — depicts «The Homage paid by William II of Germany and the other German princes to the Emperor on the occasion of the Sixtieth anniversary of his Reign» (1908).

The *wedding chamber* of Francis Joseph and Elizabeth also seems to confirm this man's melancholy destiny, recalling the great love he had for his lovely wife who was however unable to tolerate the stuffy, oppressive atmosphere of the court. The fine furniture in palisander, a gift of the Viennese woodworkers, soon became nothing but a useless example of craftmanship.

Out in the large park behind the palace, the view is magnificent: the broad strip of Italian gardens, inter-

rupted by the Neptune fountain, is transformed into a lawn which is crowned by the aerial loggia known as the Gloriette. On either side, walls of trees conceal woods dotted with fountains and statues.

The general project for the gardens was designed by the Frenchman Johann Trehet who then saw his plans realized between 1695 and 1699. A half a century later, thanks to her renewed interest in the castle, Maria Theresa gave orders for a project of embellishment to be carried out, for which Prince Anton Wenzel Kaunitz provided the theme: a historical-mythological illustration of nature, not without didactic scope. In 1770 the commission was entrusted to Ferdinand von Hohenberg and in 1772 Johann Wilhelm Beyer began to sculpt the statues.

Even so Maria Theresa was reluctant to have the loggia, designed by Von Hohenberg and already part of Fischer von Erlach's original plans, built at the top of the hill. On March 3, 1773 she still wrote to her daughter Marie Antoinette: «The changes of the hill of Schönbrunn exist only on paper and will never be carried out». It was not until 1775 that the sovereign approved them, also having work begun on other projects still «on paper»: the Roman ruins and Neptune's fountain.

The Gloriette, built as a monument to celebrate Frederick the Great's defeat at Kolin (June 18, 1757) — a victory that forced the Prussians to abandon Bohemia — looks like a colonnade adorned with military trophies.

An odder monument is the imposing *Roman ruin* immersed in the green woods and inspired by the love for Romanism typical of Baroque art. Against the ruins of a powerful arch, a group of statues — the union of the Molday and Elba rivers — rises from the reeds of a basin that has

been purposely half-covered with sand, forming a particularly haunting ensemble.

The rearrangement of the park designed by Von Hohenberg also planned for the setting up of two basins decorated by Nymphs, to be set at the crossing of the main side avenues. A star-shaped basin, which was situated at the foot of the back stairs, was moved and used for the west basin.

Finally, not far from the Roman ruins, in an artificial grotto made for Maria Theresa, we can admire the nymph Hegeria — a legendary advisor of Numa Pompilio, second king of Rome, carved by Wilhelm Beyer — who lets the water of the «beautiful fountain» (schöne Brunnen) well up.

In 1780, the completion of the Neptune fountain terminated the park which then had acquired its present-day aspect.

Schönbrunn: the Nymph Hegeria,
by Wilhelm Beyer.

Schönbrunn, Wagenburg: the imperial coach (1763 ca.)
built for Franz I Stephan.

WAGENBURG

The Wagenburg or Coach Museum is situated in one of the pavilions to one side of the grand courtyard of the palace of Schönbrunn which was completely restructured at the beginning of the 1970s.

The collection is part of the Kunsthistorisches Museum and consists of an orderly display of everything regarding transportation in the Imperial Court in the period ranging from the 17th century to the end of the reign. One of the most interesting pieces is the imperial coach, built around 1763 for Emperor Francis I and used for the first time in 1764 in Frankfurt for the coronation of Joseph II Emperor.

Particularly striking is the hearse constructed in the court workshops between 1876 and 1877 and employed solely for imperial funerals. It was used for Rudolf, Elizabeth and, for the last time, for Francis Joseph.

Schönbrunn, Wagenburg: the personal carriage (1815 ca.) of Francis I.

ST. MARX FRIEDHOF

Isolated from the main traffic routes and almost suffocated by the imposing viaduct recently built, the Cemetery of St. Marx, which was used until 1874, is now more of a park than a cemetery, especially charming in May, when the hundreds of blossoming lilacs impart a touch of melancholy to the atmosphere. There are various illustrious tombs here, including that of the sculptor, Georg Raphael Donner, but it is famous above all because this is where Wolfgang Amadeus Mozart was buried.

When this great son of Salzburg died on December 5, 1791, at the age of 35, his wife Costanza could offer nothing better than a third-class funeral in the common grave. All of seventeen years passed before Costanza thought of setting up a tomb for her husband.

A rather mannered weeping angel marks the burial place of the great musician, identified on the basis of rather vague testimony, for his remains have never been recuperated.

ZENTRAL-FRIEDHOF

The great urban expansion of Vienna in the 19th century made it indispensable to locate a new municipal cemetery in a more peripherical zone, in what was then the suburb of Simmering.

Designed in 1865 by the architects Bluntschi and Mylius and installed in 1874 with all the pomp which was characteristic of the Ringstrasse at the time, the Zentralfriedhof is a unique ensemble of history, art and customs. The principal architectural elements, such as the monumental Entrance and above all the imposing Art Nouveau church (1907-1910), were designed by the architect Max Hegele. Vienna's most famous mayor, Karl Lueger, is

St. Marx Friedhof:
the funeral monument to Mozart.

Zentralfriedhof: the Church.

Zentralfriedhof: funeral monuments to Johannes Brahms and Johann Strauss.

buried in the crypt of the church, while the crypt of the Federal Presidents of the Republic of Austria is in front of the church.

Returning along the tree-lined avenue which leads back to the principal entrance to the cemetery, the visitor encounters the areas reserved for the burials of «Austria's Great», real open-air mausoleums of the most prestigious men of culture and politicians of the country. Grouped together here, in a silent circle, are also the remains of the greatest musicians of our times: Ludwig van Beethoven, Franz Schubert, Johannes Brahms, Johann Strauss father and son, and still others, to end up with Hugo Wolf.

KIRCHE AM STEINHOF

Masterpiece of Art Nouveau, Otto Wagner built this church between 1904 and 1907 as part of the complex of the insane asylum of the region of Lower Austria, now the psychiatric clinic of Vienna.

In this church dedicated to St. Leopold, Wagner's standing as a modern architect was confirmed, attentive to the function and the functionality of the building. He studied in detail the problems that would have been presented by the specific type of persons for whom the building was intended, in an attempt to find the most suitable solutions.

Even from a distance the church strikes the visitor on account of its copper dome and the impression of simplicity and elegance furnished by the structure as a whole, with its walls faced with slabs of white marble, apparently held in place by nails, an ornamental feature the architect had already used for the Postsparkasse.

The interior, flooded with light, is enriched by the polychrome stained-glass windows designed by Kolo Moser, while the large mosaic behind the high altar is by Rudolf Jettmar.

The Church of St. Leopold am Steinhof.

St. Leopold am Steinhof, the mosaic of the high altar.

HEERESGE-SCHICHTLICHES MUSEUM

In the middle of the 19th century Francis Joseph decided to move the old city arsenal, accepting the plans for the new complex elaborated by the architects Eduard von der Null and August von Siccardsburg. Inside the new arsenal, situated not far beyond the Belvedere, a building, designed by Theophil Hansen, was erected to house the museum of the military history of Austria. The collections provide an extensive survey which ranges from the Thirty Years War (1618-1648) up to World War I.

HUNDERTWASSER-HAUS (HUNDERTWASSER HOUSE)

Vienna has a fine tradition when it comes to housing. Therefore, it was entirely natural to commission a modern artist, Friedensreich Hundertwasser to design his version of the apartment house with full freedom. The *Hundertwasserhaus*, located in the 3rd district at the corner of *Kegelgasse* and *Löwengasse* is an original contribution to urban renewal. The purpose of this building is to restore the dialogue with nature which is viewed as an equal partner. In fact, there are many plants and trees on the roof, balconies and terraces. The building was completed in 1985 after twenty years of con-

Heeresgeschichtliches Museum: the facade, the atrium and the 17th-century room.

struction. It is intriguingly audacious thanks to the several innovative solutions its architect selected: colors, outside walls that are not uniformly smooth, differently shaped windows, etc.. Just a short distance away, at n. 13 *Unteren Weissgerberstrasse* is the *Kunsthaus Wien*, a museum containing many many works by Hundertwasser. This museum is a "bastion against the false order of straight lines", is uneven floor is a "symphony for the feet."

Hundertwasserhaus

Kunsthaus Wien

PRATER

Today the Prater is an enormous public park which spreads out over more than 1700 hectares between the Danube and the Donaukanal. Once upon a time this vast area was a Hapsburg hunting reserve which Joseph II opened to the public in 1766. Cafés and restaurants immediately began to spring up along the main boulevard.

In 1873 the architect Lothar Abel reviewed the set-up with an eye to accommodating what was to be the greatest world fair realized up to then. Vienna and the Empire wanted to show the world their industrial might.

It was a disaster. Nine days after the inauguration of the World Fair (May 1, 1873) a tremendous crash in the Viennese stock exchange brought the economy of the country to its knees, and it stagnated for almost twenty years. To top things off, an epidemy of cholera broke out in June and kept many visitors away from the Fair.

The Viennese love this place for entertainment and rendezvous, above all on Sunday afternoons, when children comfortably ride on the Liliputbahn, the Lilliputian railroad. The Volksprater, known also as Wurstelprater, is dominated by the gigantic *Riesenrad*, the ferris wheel which, after the high spire of St. Stephen's, has

The «Riesenrad» in the Prater.

Attractions of all kinds in the large ▶ Amusement Park of the Prater.

become the second symbol of Vienna. Sixty-four meters high and sixty-one meters in diameter, it was built in 1897 by the English engineer Basset for the Vienna World Fair. From its cabins, which take a full turn every twenty minutes, one can get a truly unforgettable panorama of the city.

DONAUPARK

This modern park which was initially set up as the site for the International Garden Show of Vienna in 1964, covers a vast area situated between an arm of the old course of the Danube and the broad artificial canal through which the river flows today.

The disastrous flood of 1862 which struck the eastern part of the city, including the Prater and Leopoldstadt, convinced the town council to prepare a project for its canalization. Carried out between 1870 and 1875, works included a spacious reservoir, a wide canal for navigation and a smaller canal which would flow along the old course, skirting the city and at least in part preserving its original appearance; the old principal bend would thus be cut off to the east.

Surrounded by the green of a large variety of tall trees are areas with sport facilities, playgrounds for children, bicycle paths, minigolf, refreshment centers. Music is also provided by a small orchestra which plays outside. The Donauturm (Danube Tower), a respectable 252 metres high, rises up over the park. It was built in 1964 on the example of the television towers present in so many other cities. Swift elevators rise up to the revolving café restaurant, 170 meters up, from which there is a superb panoramic view of the Danube and the city.

UNO-CITY

In the southern corner of the Donaupark, near the Reichsbrücke (Imperial Bridge), the Austrian government has established the Vienna International Center for the United Nations and International Atomic Energy Agency, commonly called by the abbreviation «UNO-City». Designed by the architect Johann Staber and begun in 1973, it was finished in 1979. The complex, which has a novel curved form, includes a well-equipped world center for congresses as well as numerous buildings and sectors of UNO.

Amusements in the Donaupark.

UNO-City. ▶

HEILIGENSTADT

This small village, which by now has become a suburb of Vienna, an old wine center, is best known for the fact that Ludwig van Beethoven lived here at various times.

At Pfarrplatz no. 2, next to the parish church, of medieval origins, is a simple 18th-century building where the musician spent a summer. The writer Franz Grillparzer (1791-1872) tells how his mother had rented the apartment next to Beethoven's, from which it was separated by a hall. The young Grillparzer loved to listen to the master playing from behind the door. But when this innocent eavesdropping was discovered, the piano of the touchy musician stayed silent for the rest of the summer.

Heiligenstadt: Pfarrplatz with the parish church of S. James.

Heiligenstadt: Beethoven's house.

GRINZING

An old popular village of vine-growers situated on the lower slopes of the Wienerwald, it did not become part of the XIX district of Vienna until 1891. Even though it was destroyed more than once by the Turks and the French, various old buildings such as the Trummel Hof and the Altes Haus managed to survive. It is now a typical tourist center, a destination chosen for its traditional Heurigen and the gay picturesque atmosphere of its animated streets. The Heurigen are the typical wine-shops which sell new wine (the term derives from «heurig», meaning of this year, of the current vintage) and are often run by the producers themselves. Traditionally they are marked by a pine branch hung outside or a painted metal sign. Food, drink, and the traditional Viennese music (Schrammel-Musik) played by the typical quartet which generally consists of lyre, violin, guitar and accordion. But above all an evening of real Viennese life.

Famous men rest in the cemetery of Grinzing, including Heinrich Ferstel, who designed the Votivkirche (1828-1883), and Gustav Mahler (1860-1911), great composer and for years the Director of the Vienna State Opera.

*Grinzing: Trummel Hof,
a very old Heurigen.*

*Grinzing: the Reinprecht Heurigen
in typical Biedermeier style.*

Grinzing: Heurigen.

KAHLENBERG

The name of this hill is almost synonymous with the memorable defeat of the Turks who had besieged Vienna in 1683. The night of September 11th, the imperial troops commanded by Charles V, duke of Lorraine and the Polish troops under King John Sobiesky joined forces at Klosterneuburg and launched an attack by night, driving the Turks from the height of St. Joseph's Berg, as Kahlenberg was then called.

On Sunday, September 12th, the imperial forces rushed down from the heights of the hill towards the plain and the city, overrunning the entrenched field positions which were besieging Vienna. The battle broke up into various separate encounters, scattered over a vast zone, and neither the imperial generals — and much less Kara Mustafà, supreme Turkish commander — succeeded in coordinating the strategy. When the Christian troops penetrated the camp of the Turkish vizier himself, he retreated in disorderly haste. It was 5:30 in the afternoon: the siege of Vienna had come to an end.

Kahlenberg can be reached via the Hohenstrasse, a splendid panoramic route that winds through the hills of the Wienerwald. At the top of the hill a spacious terrace offers a marvelous view of Vienna and the Danube. Nearby is the 18th-century Josefskirche, finished in 1734. Relics of the battle of 1683 and mementos of the Polish king are exhibited in the Sobiesky chapel. Inside, in memory of Sobiesky's soldiers, there is also a copy of the Black Madonna of Czestochowa, the most venerated image in Poland.

Leopoldsberg: Leopoldskirche.

◀ Kahlenberg: the church of S. Joseph.

◀ Kahlenberg: panoramic view of the slopes of the Wienerwald and Vienna.

◀ Wienerwald.

LEOPOLDSBERG

The Hohenstrasse ends here, on the cliff of Leopoldsberg, the easternmost rampart of the Wienerwald and the Alps, which rises straight up 266 meters from the Danube below. A Babenberg castle which stood here — traces are still visible — was the residence of the dukes up to 1155, when Duke Henry II Jasomirgott moved to the area of the square Am Hof in Vienna. Margrave Leopold III Babenberg, later patron saint of Lower Austria and in particular of the city of Vienna, had lived here. In 1679 Emperor Leopold replaced the ancient Chapel of St. George, dating to the early 15th century, with the Leopoldskirche, in memory of the margrave saint. Damaged during the Turkish siege, it was finished in 1693, only to be remodelled by the Italian architect Beduzzi between 1718 and 1730. In 1945 bombs destroyed about a third.

From the square, the eye sweeps over the Danube and the eastern quarters of the city, to the distant Hungarian plain.

KLOSTERNEUBURG

The Augustiner-Chorherrenstift (Augustinian Abbey) was founded in 1100 by Margrave Leopold III Babenberg (the Saint) and a curious legend is connected with its origins: a gust of wind is said to have blown the veil from the head of Agnes, the margrave's wife, while they were observing the underlying plain from their Leopoldsberg castle, and Leopold vowed he would build a monastery where the veil came to rest. In 1683 the abbey was damaged by fire. Charles VI, entrusting the reconstruction projects to the Milanese Donato Felice dall'Allio and the famous Josef Fischer von Erlach, hoped to promote an ambitious project of a complex along the lines of the Escorial. The project provided for groups of buildings with domes in the form of the crowns of the Hapsburg family. But when Charles VI died, in 1743, only two domes had been completed. Not till much later, between 1836 and 1842, did the architect Joseph Kornhäusel build another wing to the ensemble, partially completing the interrupted work.

The monastery church, consecrated in 1136, stands on the foundations of an older building. It was often remodelled and is now a sort of combined neo-Romanesque and neo-Gothic style.

The Baroque interior is the result of three different periods of work between 1634 and 1730. The two towers in neo-Gothic style on either side of the facade are by

◀ *Klosterneuburg: panoramic view of the Augustinian Abbey.*

Perchtoldsdorf: the Pestsäule and the Wehrturm.

◀ *Klosterneuburg: the neo-Gothic towers of the Stiftskirche.*

Friedrich Schmidt (1890).

Various masterpieces are to be found in the Abbey. Of particular note is the famous Verdun Altar, a finely executed work in enamel, consisting of 51 Biblical scenes, made in 1181 by Nicholas of Verdun, the master of the Three Kings reliquary in Cologne.

PERCHTOLDSDORF

This old village of vine-growers also preserves outstanding monuments of the past. The traditional Trinity Column, designed by Johann Bernhard Fischer von Erlach in 1713, stands in the principal square, flanked by the imposing Wehrturm erected in the first half of the 15th century, when the church was transformed into a military installation. Today the tower is the symbol of the town. Also to be noted is the parish church, St. Augustin, dating to 1340, with a solemn tripartite interior and a fine high altar in Baroque style.

123

MÖDLING

An old Babenberg town, the center has been perfectly preserved.

The traditional Trinity Column, or Plague Column, dated 1714, stands in the main square. Overlooking the square is also a Renaissance Rathaus (Town Hall) of 1548 as well as a number of Gothic-Renaissance buildings. At number 79 of the Hauptstrasse is the Hafnerhaus, a lovely house with a late Gothic court with two tiers of arches, where Beethoven, who lived here between 1818 and 1819, composed his «Messa Solenne».

SCHLOSS LIECHTENSTEIN

Not far from Mödling is the castle of Liechtenstein, the romantic 19th-century reconstruction of an old medieval fortress. The original citadel was built in 1165 for the «troubador» Ulrich von Liechtenstein. Prince Jean I of Liechtenstein bought the ruins in 1808 and had a castle built on the basis of the neo-Gothic canons in vogue early in the 19th century. Facing the fort is a rotonda with classic columns, the Husarentempel built in remembrance of the seven Hussars who had saved the prince in the battle of Essling (Aspern) in 1809.

LAXENBURG

Three castles which belonged to the Hapsburgs stand in the vast park of this site: the Blauer Hof, made for Maria Theresa and transformed around 1752 by Pacassi into a new large architectural complex; the Altes Schloss, once a castle protected by an artificial pond (despite the numerous transformations it was subjected to up into the 18th century, traces of the Gothic buildings which overlooked the left court are still evident);and the romantic Franzenburg set on an island between 1798 and 1836. In April of 1854 Francis Joseph and Elizabeth spent their brief honeymoon in Laxenburg, the Hapsburg summer residence. It was here, on August 21, 1858, that Rudolf, the heir to the throne who was to die tragically in Mayerling, first saw the light of day.

MAYERLING

The visitor will seek in vain for what is perhaps the most famous hunting pavilion in the world, for not the slightest trace remains.

On January 30, 1889, the body of Rudolf, son of the emperor and only heir to the throne, was found in a corner room of the lodge. Next to him lay the lifeless body of his mistress, the baroness Maria Vetsera. A drama which moved and perturbed the world and which, exaggerated by the lies which resulted from the frenzied attempts of Francis Joseph and his police to maintain secrecy, has long since become legend.

In this case more than ever one can say that rivers of ink have been used in trying to come to a conclusion, but very little seems to have been clarified.

The prince had obviously committed suicide with a revolver shot in his head, while there are doubts as to the cause of Maria Vetsera's death, for the documents of the autopsy, if there ever was one, were never found.

◀ *Mödling: the Trinity Column.*

◀ *Schloss Liechtenstein.*

◀ *Schloss Laxenburg.*

Mayerling: the chapel of the convent.

Mayerling: old «shed».

The tomb of Maria Vetsera in Heiligenkreuz.

Was it because he was in imminent danger of seeing himself publicly unmasked as a participant in the so-called «Hungarian plot», or was it a fit of depression caused by the insignificant controlled life in which he was imprisoned that drove Rudolf to seek death? Or was it the impossibility of crowning a great love, or the extreme gesture of a physique weakened by morphine and by the vein of madness in his maternal family line? Or lastly, as the latest hypothesis suggests, was it the only way out of an attempt at abortion, on Maria's part but organized by Rudolf, which had resulted in the tragic death of the girl? We do not know what caused the prince to put an end to his life and we may never know. The zeal of the Hapsburg police managed to make almost all the documents on the case vanish.

Today the Mayerling of Rudolf and Maria no longer exists. The emperor gave orders to demolish the hunting lodge and it was replaced by a Carmelite convent.

The present chapel was built on the site of the tragedy, and two walls of Rudolf's room were incorporated in the structure.

On the night of February 1, the body of Maria Vetsera was secretly transported to Heiligenkreuz and hastily buried in the abbey cemetery, where it still rests, protected from prying eyes.

HEILINGENKREUZ

The Cistercian abbey complex of Heiligenkreuz was founded in 1155 by Leopold III Babenberg (the Saint) on the advice of his son Otto, a Cistercian monk. The name of the abbey, remodeled in Baroque style in the 17th-18th centuries on a project by Domenico Canevale, is due to the presence there of a fragment of the true Cross which the founder's nephew, Duke Leopold IV, had brought back from the Holy Land in 1183 and donated to the convent. Another relic preserved in the abbey is a thorn from the crown of thorns, which St. Louis sent as a gift to the duke of Austria. The main courtyard is arcaded and contains the Josefsbrunnen and the Trinity Column, designed by G. Giuliani in 1739. Facing it is the severe Romanesque facade of the church (1260) crowned by a 17th-century tower. The tripartite interior has tall clustered piers and is illuminated by enormous three-light windows with 14th-century stained glass, and terminates in a spacious and luminous choir (1260), masterpiece of Austrian Gothic. Of particular interest is the Cloister (1220-1250) with over 300 columns in fine red marble. and decorated with two large groups of the Washing of Feet by Giuliani. The Stiftsmuseum across from the church contains models and studies by Giuliani, stained glass, weapons, prehistoric collections and examples of local folklore; in the picture gallery, 15th-century German work and examples of the Austrian Baroque (Altomonte).

Heiligenkreuz: the facade of the abbey church and the Trinity Column.

Heiligenkreuz: the interior of the abbey church.

Heiligenkreuz: corridor in the cloister.

CONTENTS